BRAIN QUEST®

KINDERGARTEN WORKBOOK

Written by Lisa Trumbauer
Consulting Editor: Kimberly Oliver

Workman Publishing • New York

This book belongs to:

First Name

Last Name

ISBN 978-1-5235-1734-3

New and updated text by Jen Agresta and Jennifer Szymanski; educational review by Anne Haywood, Rosa Fernandez, and Peg Keiner

Illustrations by George Ulrich, Kimble Mead, Emily Bolam, Jamie Smith, and Scott Dubar, with cover illustrations by Edison Yan

Workbook series design by Raquel Jaramillo

30th Anniversary Edition Revision produced for Workman by WonderLab Group, LLC, and Fan Works Design, LLC.

Workman books are available at special discounts when purchased in bulk for premiums and sales promotions as well as for fundraising or educational use. Special editions or book excerpts can also be created to specification. For details, please contact special.markets@hbgusa.com.

WORKMAN, BRAIN QUEST, and IT'S FUN TO BE SMART! are registered trademarks of Workman Publishing Co., Inc., a subsidiary of Hachette Book Group, Inc.

Workman Publishing Co., Inc., a subsidiary of Hachette Book Group, Inc.
1290 Avenue of the Americas
New York, NY 10104
workman.com • brainquest.com

Distributed in the United Kingdom by Hachette Book Group, UK, Carmelite House, 50 Victoria Embankment, London, EC4Y 0DZ.

Distributed in Europe by Hachette Livre, 58 rue Jean Bleuzen, 92 178 Vanves Cedex, France.

Printed in China on responsibly sourced paper.

First printing April 2023
10 9 8 7 6 5 4 3 2 1

Dear Parents and Caregivers,

Learning is an adventure—a quest for knowledge. At Brain Quest we strive to guide children on that quest, to keep them motivated and curious, and to give them the confidence they need to do well in school and beyond. We're excited to partner with you and your child as they take this first step in their lifelong knowledge quest.

BRAIN QUEST WORKBOOKS are designed to enrich children's understanding in all content areas by reinforcing the basics and previewing future learning. These are not textbooks, but rather true workbooks, and are best used to reinforce curricular concepts learned at school. Each workbook aligns to national and state learning standards and is written in consultation with an award-winning grade-level teacher.

In kindergarten, children learn about how letters combine to form sounds and words. They build their vocabulary by reading simple words and learning sight words. Children build pre-math and critical-thinking skills as they explore the numbers 1 through 12, and learn about shapes, colors, patterns, and more.

We're excited that BRAIN QUEST WORKBOOKS will play an integral role in your child's educational adventure. So let the learning—and the fun—begin!

It's fun to be smart!®

—The editors of Brain Quest

HOW TO USE THIS BOOK

Welcome to the Brain Quest Kindergarten Workbook!

Encourage your child to complete the workbook at their own pace. Guide them to approach the work with a **growth mindset**, the idea that our abilities can change and grow with effort. Reinforce this by praising effort and problem-solving and explaining that mistakes are part of learning.

The **opening page** of each section has a note for parents and caregivers and another note just for kids.

Notes to children give learners a preview of each section.

Notes to parents highlight key skills and give suggestions for helping with each section.

Guide your child to place a sticker here to get excited about learning.

233

MATCHING AND SORTING

Matching means finding things that are alike. Sorting means putting things that are alike together. Let's find out what we can sort and match!

PARENTS Matching and sorting helps learners pay attention to details and organize visual information. They identify attributes of objects—shapes, colors, sizes, and more. You can reinforce matching socks or sorting silverware. Ask: How are these objects alike? What is different?

PLACE A STICKER HERE

For additional resources, visit www.BrainQuest.com/kindergarten

Read the directions aloud if needed. Encourage your child to work as independently as possible.

Get your child talking! Ask about the images they see and connections between the workbook and their lives.

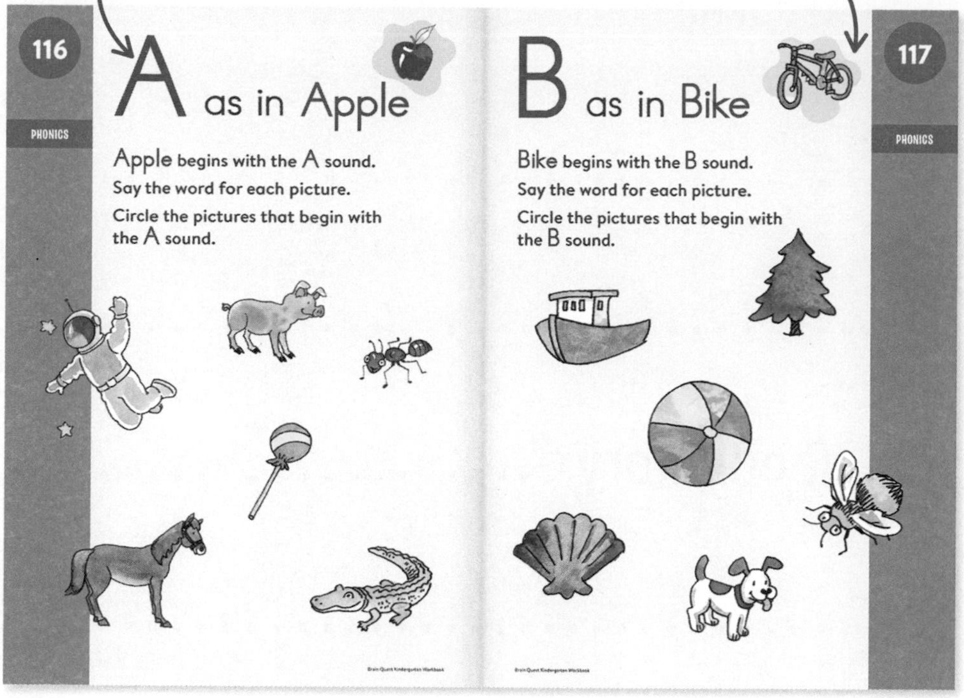

Cut out the Brain Quest **Mini-Deck** from the back to play and learn on the go!

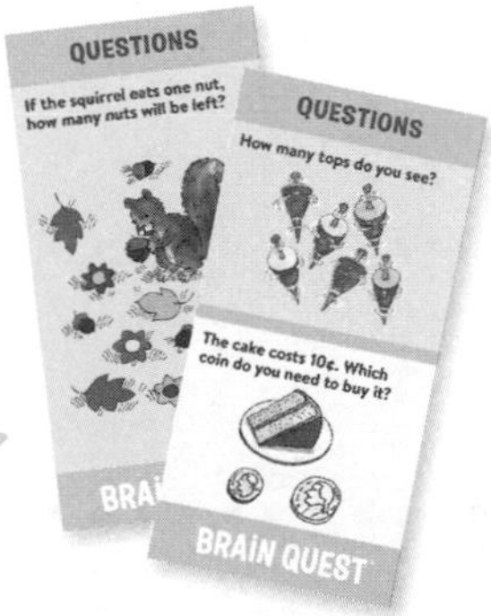

After each chapter, have your child place a sticker on the **progress map** to mark their achievement.

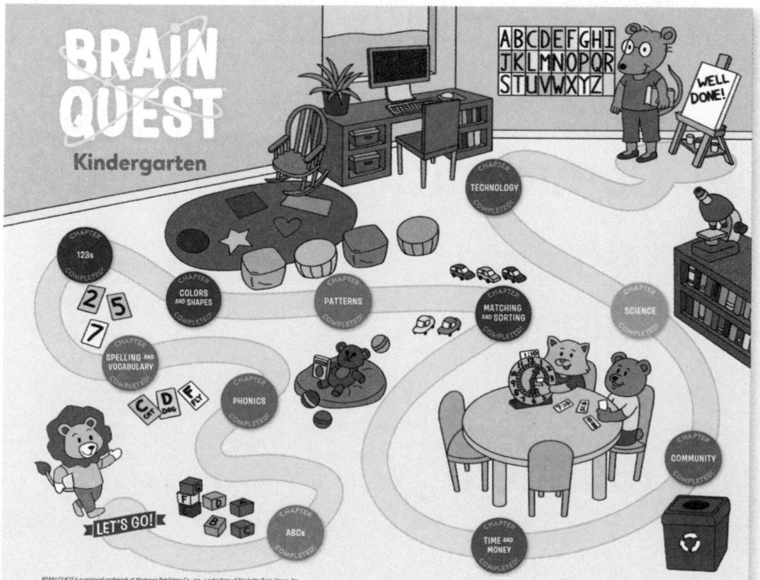

Encourage your child to use stickers to decorate the **certificate.** Hang it up when it's complete!

CONTENTS

ABCs 7

Phonics 115

Spelling and Vocabulary 155

123s 169

Colors and Shapes 209

Patterns 225

Matching and Sorting 233

Time and Money 247

Community 265

Science 281

Technology 301

Brain Quest Extras 309

ABCs

You will practice writing letters. As you work on each letter, try to find things around you that start with that letter. Are you ready to get started?
AAA
BBB
CCC
AAA
BB

PARENTS During kindergarten, children learn the alphabet and practice writing letters. Children don't naturally learn letters straight from A to Z, so feel free to jump around in this section. Start with letters that are interesting to your learner, like the first letter of their name, a pet, or a favorite color.

PLACE A STICKER HERE

For additional resources, visit www.BrainQuest.com/kindergarten

Fun with A

Help the **astronaut** find the **alligator**!

Color the spaces with A and a green.

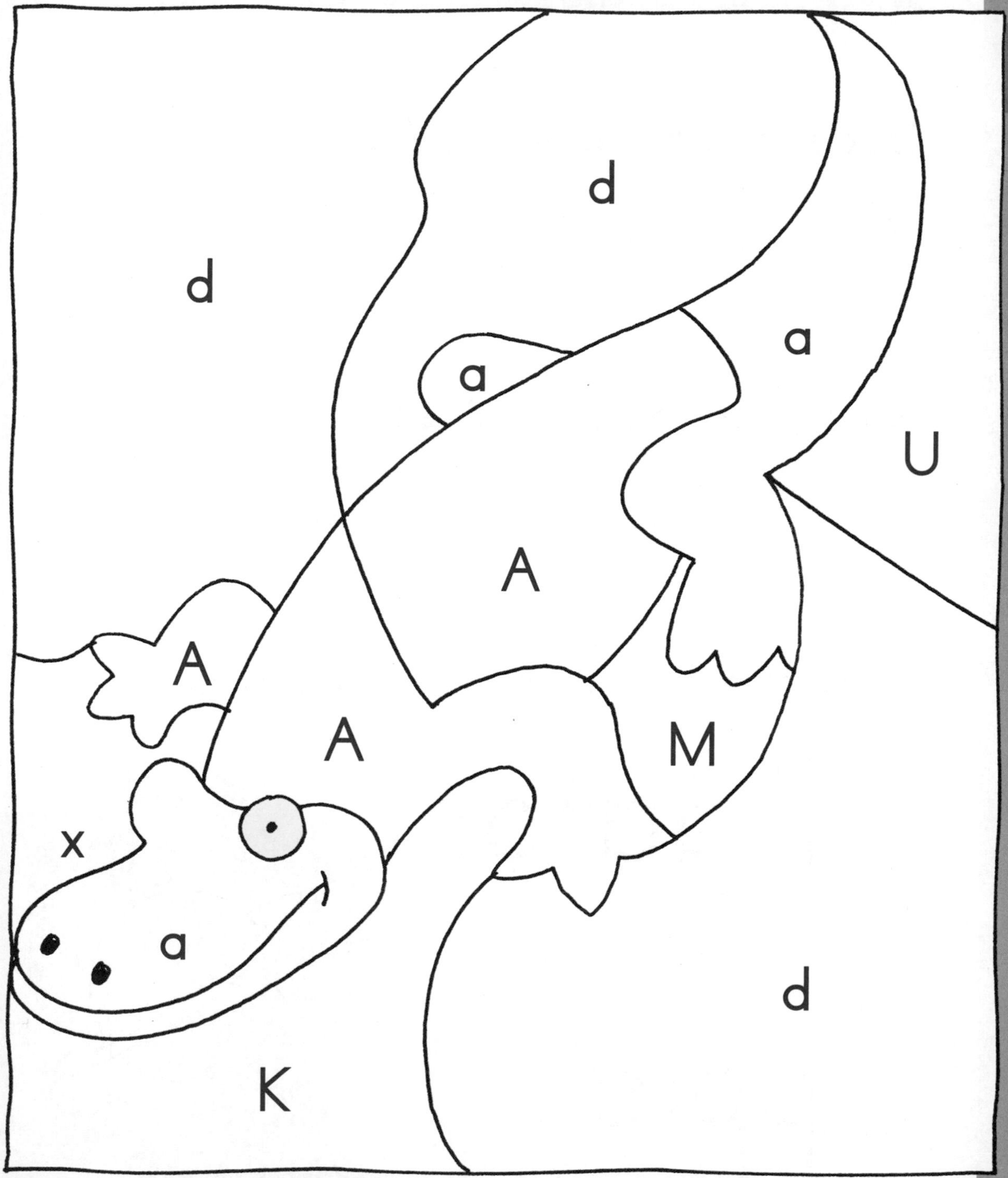

What animal do you see?

A a

Trace the capital letter A.

A A A A A A

Now write the capital letter A.

Trace the A to complete each word.

Alligator

Apple

Ari

The **alligator** is floating with the **astronaut**!

Trace the lowercase letter a.

a a a a a a a

Now write the lowercase letter a.

Trace the a to complete each word.

astronaut

at

ant

12

ABCs

Fun with B

Color all the **butterflies** and **bubbles** on the bush.

The boy is blowing bubbles!
Color the bubbles with B or b.

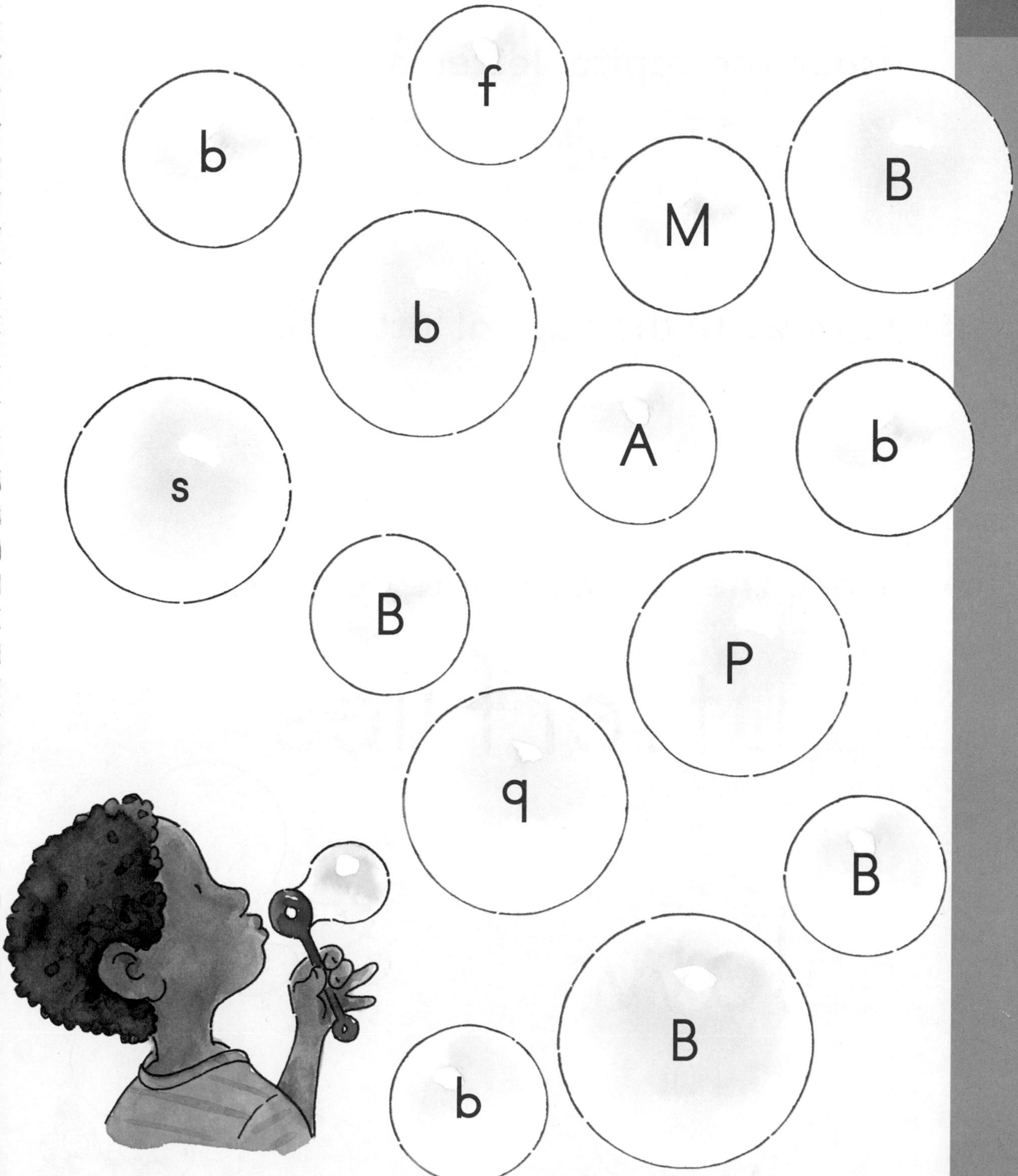

B b

Trace the capital letter B.

B B B B B B

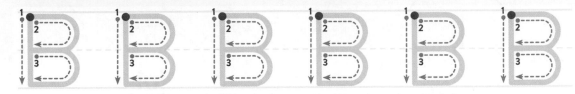

Now write the capital letter B.

Trace the B to complete each word.

Butterflies

Blow

Billy

The **butterflies** are chasing the **bubbles**!

Trace the lowercase letter b.

b b b b b b b

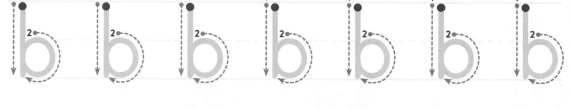

Now write the lowercase letter b.

Trace the b to complete each word.

bubbles

ball

about

Fun with C

Help the **cat** find her way to the **castle.**

Follow the cat!

Draw a line down the path with C and c.

Cc

Trace the capital letter C.

C C C C C C

Now write the capital letter C.

Trace the C to complete each word.

Cat

Caleb

Car

The **cat** will be cozy in the **castle**!

Trace the lowercase letter c.

c c c c c c c

Now write the lowercase letter c.

Trace the c to complete each word.

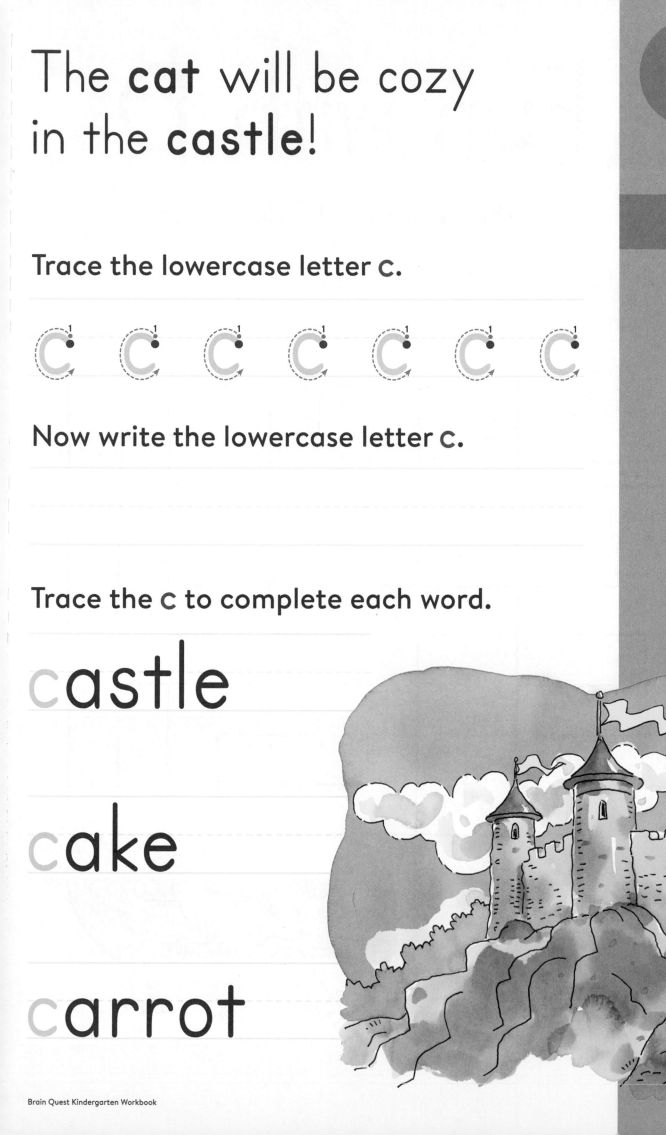

castle

cake

carrot

Fun with D

Help the **duck** find the **dinosaurs.**

Welcome to the pond!
Circle the animals with D and d.

D d

Trace the capital letter D.

D D D D D D

Now write the capital letter D.

Trace the D to complete each word.

Dinosaur

Dylan

Delia

This **dinosaur** wants to play with the **ducks**!

Trace the lowercase letter d.

d d d d d d d

Now write the lowercase letter d.

Trace the d to complete each word.

ducks

daisy

sled

Fun with E

Help the **elephant** find the **eggs.**

Color the spaces with E and e gray.

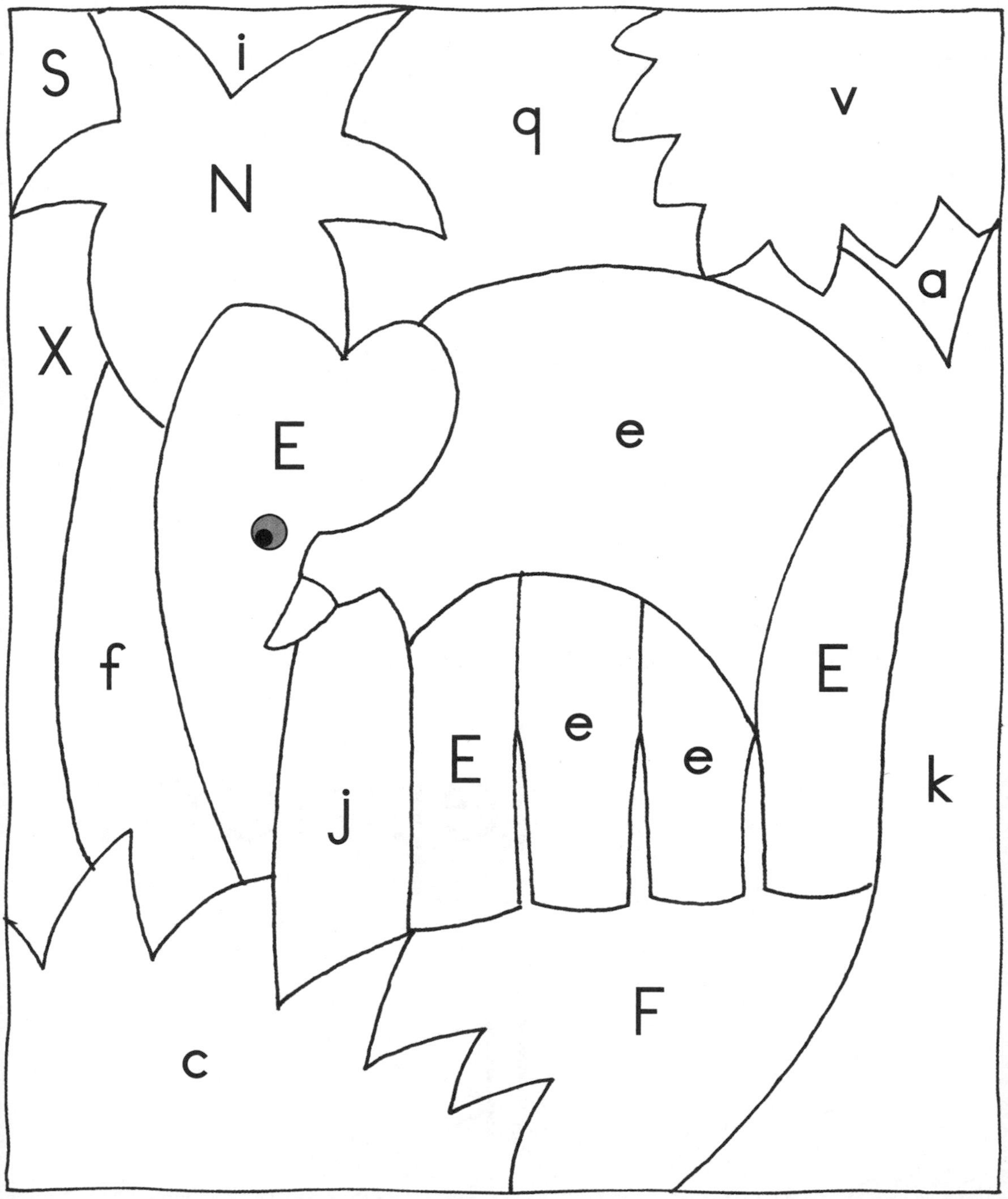

What animal do you see?

E e

Trace the capital letter E.

E E E E E E

Now write the capital letter E.

Trace the E to complete each word.

Elephant

Elk

Erin

The **elephants** are juggling the **eggs**.

Trace the lowercase letter e.

Now write the lowercase letter e.

Trace the e to complete each word.

egg

elbow

pen

Fun with F

Help the **fox** sneak onto the **farm**.

Color the shapes with F and f orange.

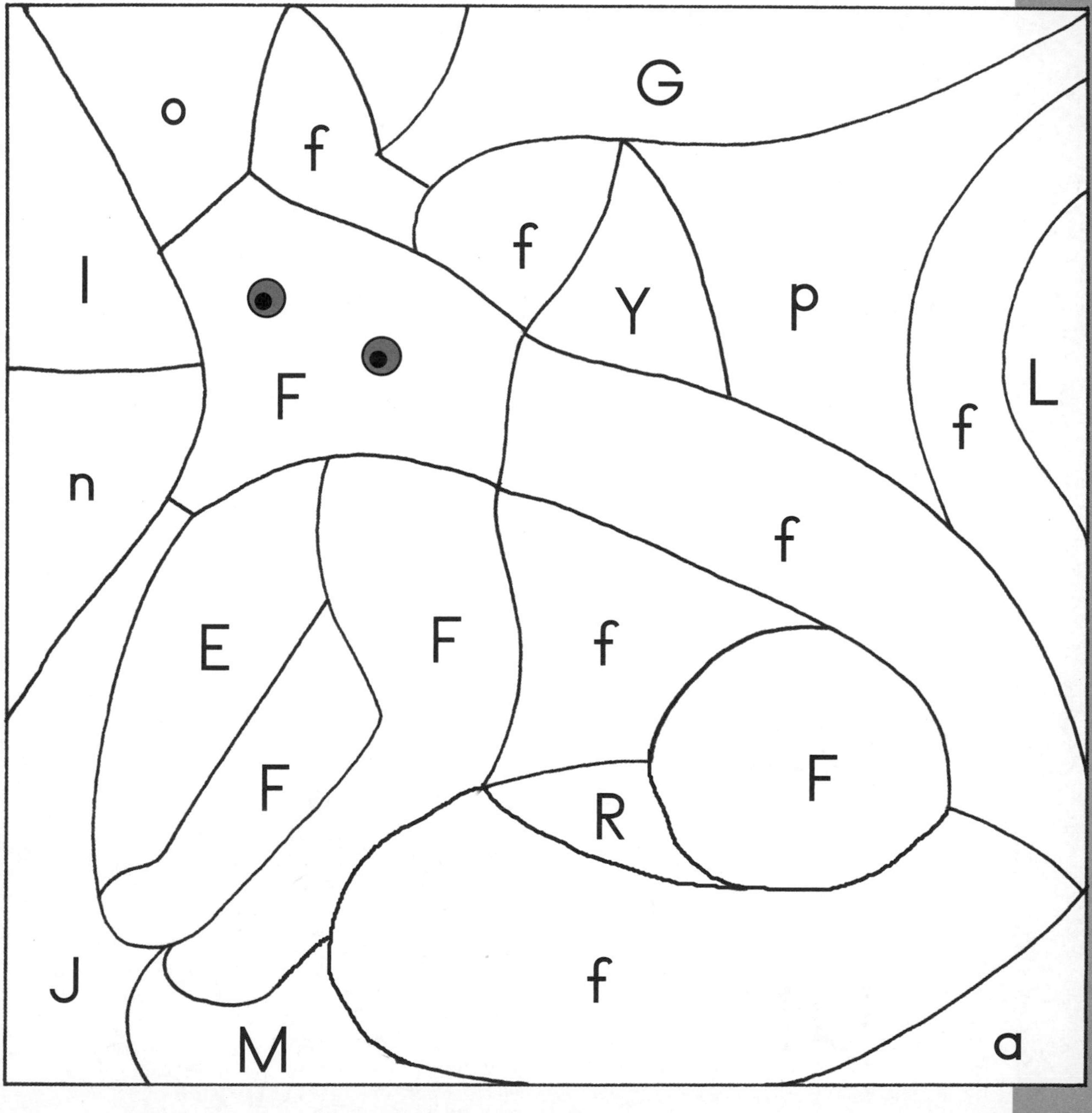

What animal do you see?

F f

Trace the capital letter F.

F F F F F F

Now write the capital letter F.

Trace the F to complete each word.

Fox

Fun

Fred

Uh-oh! The **fox** snuck onto the **farm**!

Trace the lowercase letter f.

f f f f f f

Now write the lowercase letter f.

Trace the f to complete each word.

farm

forest

before

Fun with G

Help the **ghost** find the **golfer**.

Color the shapes with G and g black.

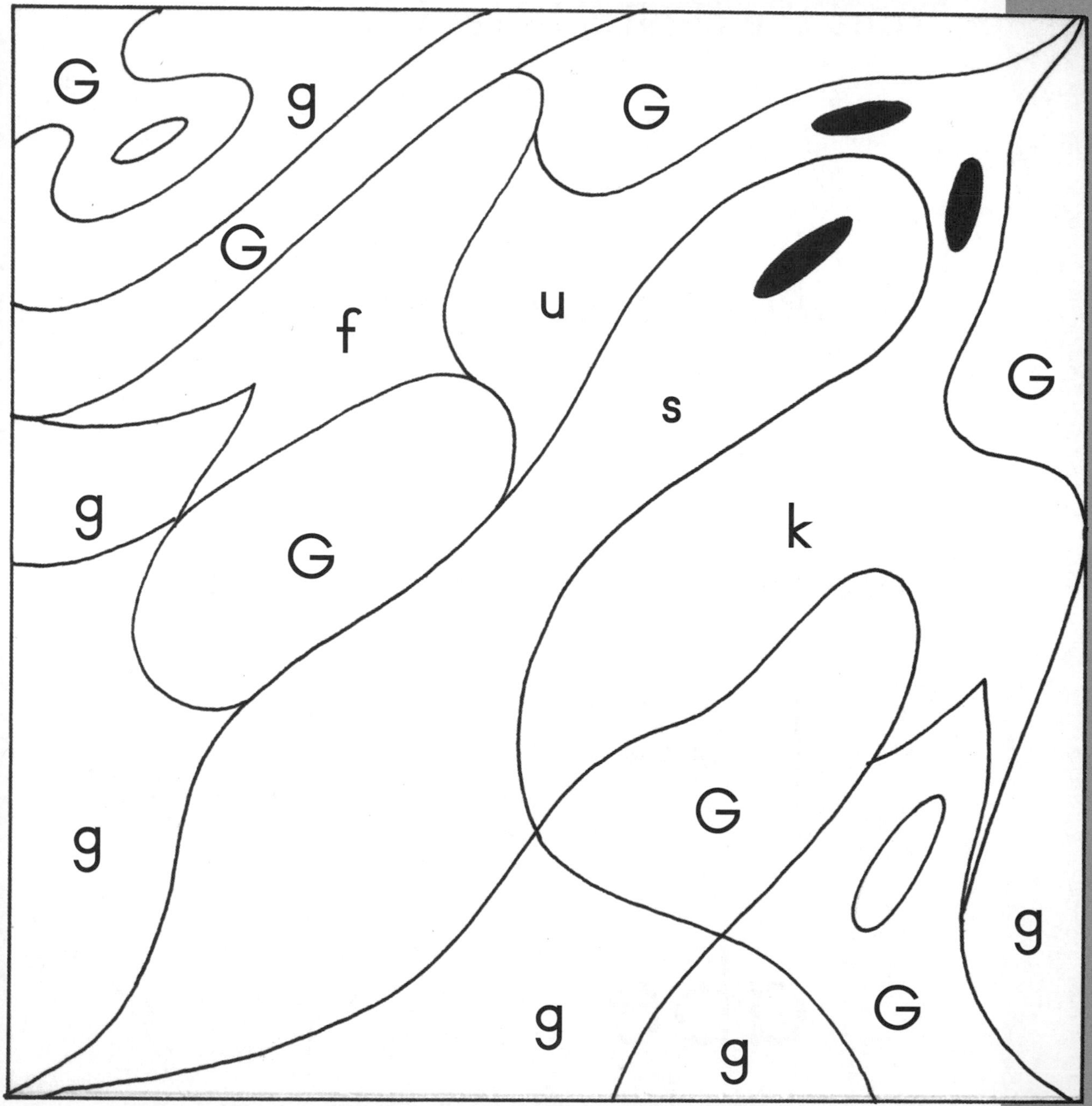

What creature do you see?

Gg

Trace the capital letter G.

G G G G G G

Now write the capital letter G.

Trace the G to complete each word.

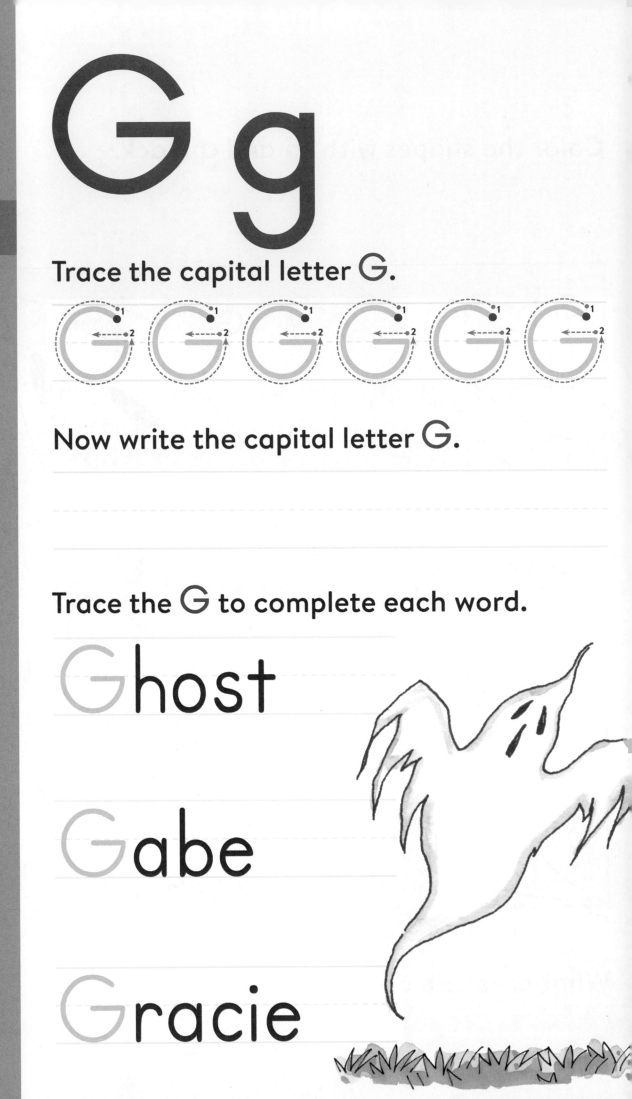

Ghost

Gabe

Gracie

The **ghost** wants to play **golf**!

Trace the lowercase letter g.

g g g g g g g

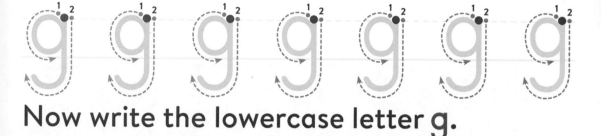

Now write the lowercase letter g.

Trace the g to complete each word.

golf

girl

ring

Fun with H

Help the **horse** get back to the **herd.**

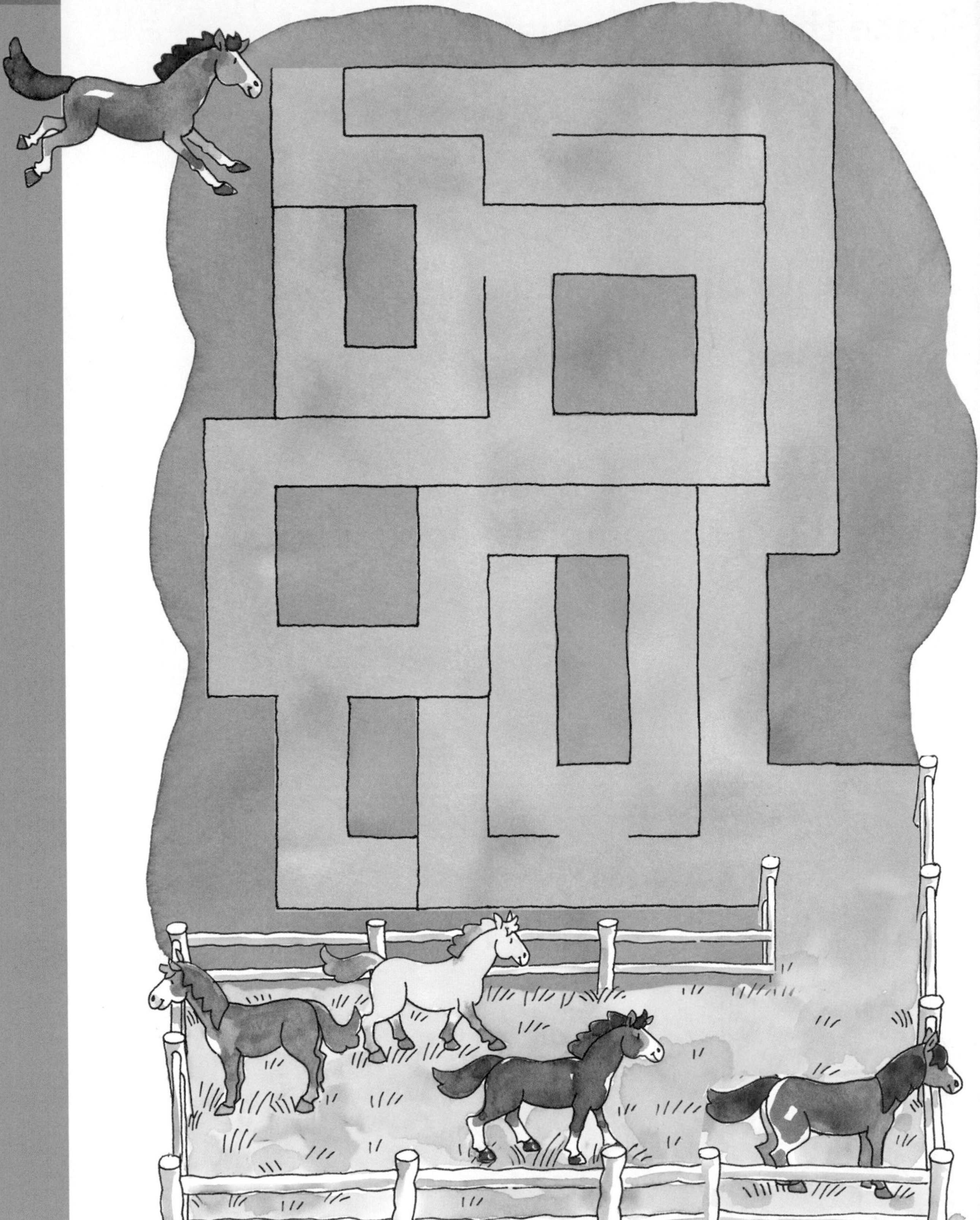

Color the horses with H and h yellow.

H h

Trace the capital letter H.

H H H H H H

Now write the capital letter H.

Trace the H to complete each word.

Horses

Hot

Hernán

The **horses** want to go to the **house**!

Trace the lowercase letter h.

h h h h h h h

Now write the lowercase letter h.

Trace the h to complete each word.

house

shell

hall

Fun with I

Help the **iguana** get to the **island**.

Color the spaces with I and i green.

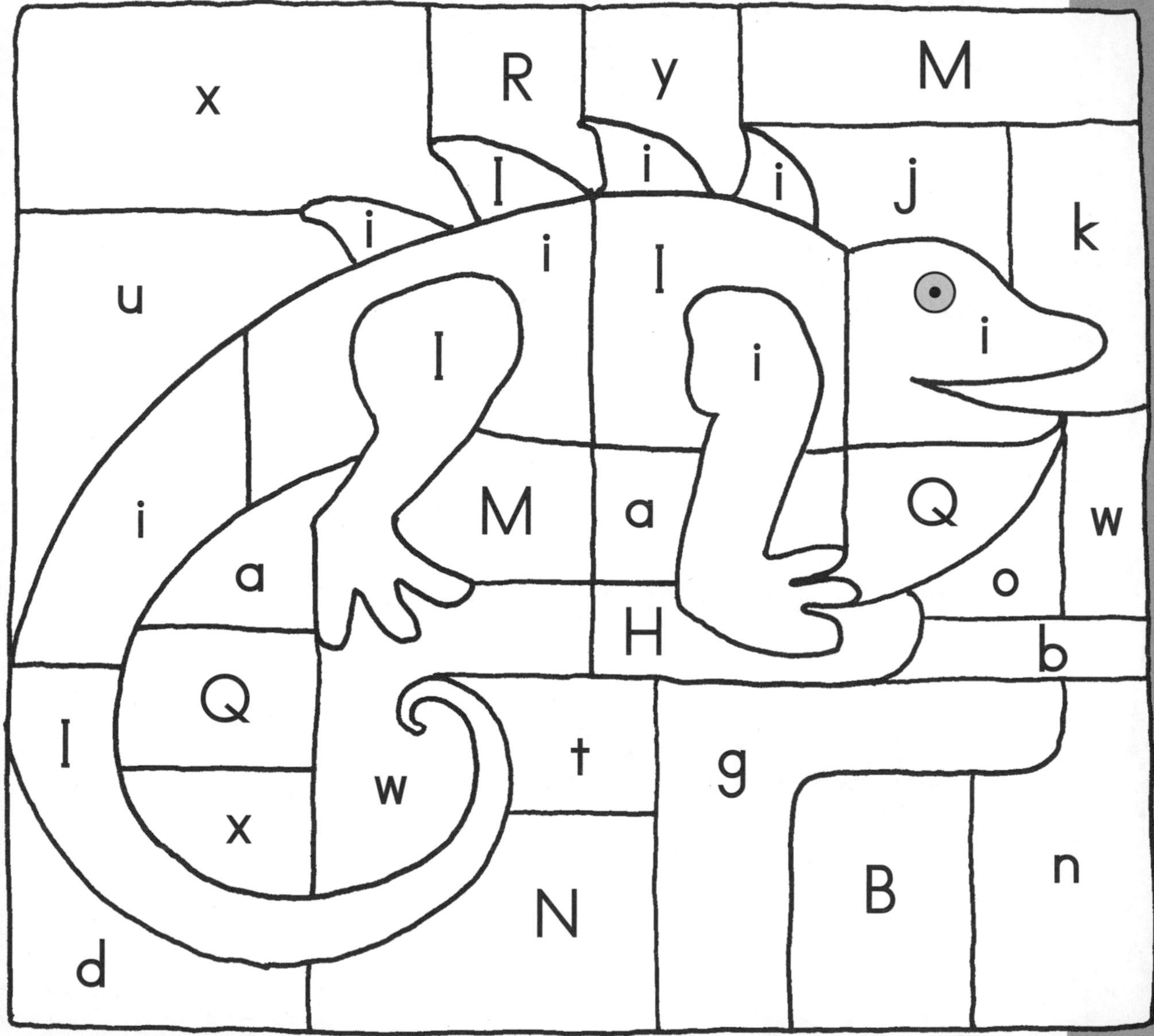

What animal do you see?

I i

Trace the capital letter I.

2 1 I 3 2 1 I 3 2 1 I 3 2 1 I 3 2 1 I 3 2 1 I 3

Now write the capital letter I.

Trace the I to complete each word.

Iguana

Issa

Inch

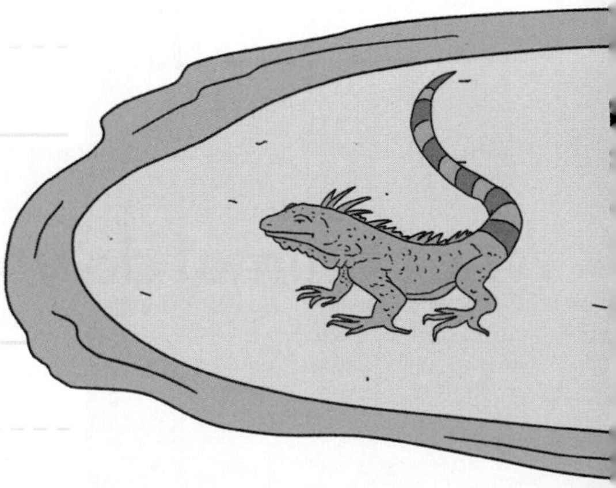

The **iguana** will be nice and warm on the **island**!

Trace the lowercase letter i.

i i i i i i i

Now write the lowercase letter i.

Trace the i to complete each word.

insect

fish

this

Fun with J

Help the **jaguar** find the **jump** rope!

Color the shapes with J and j orange.

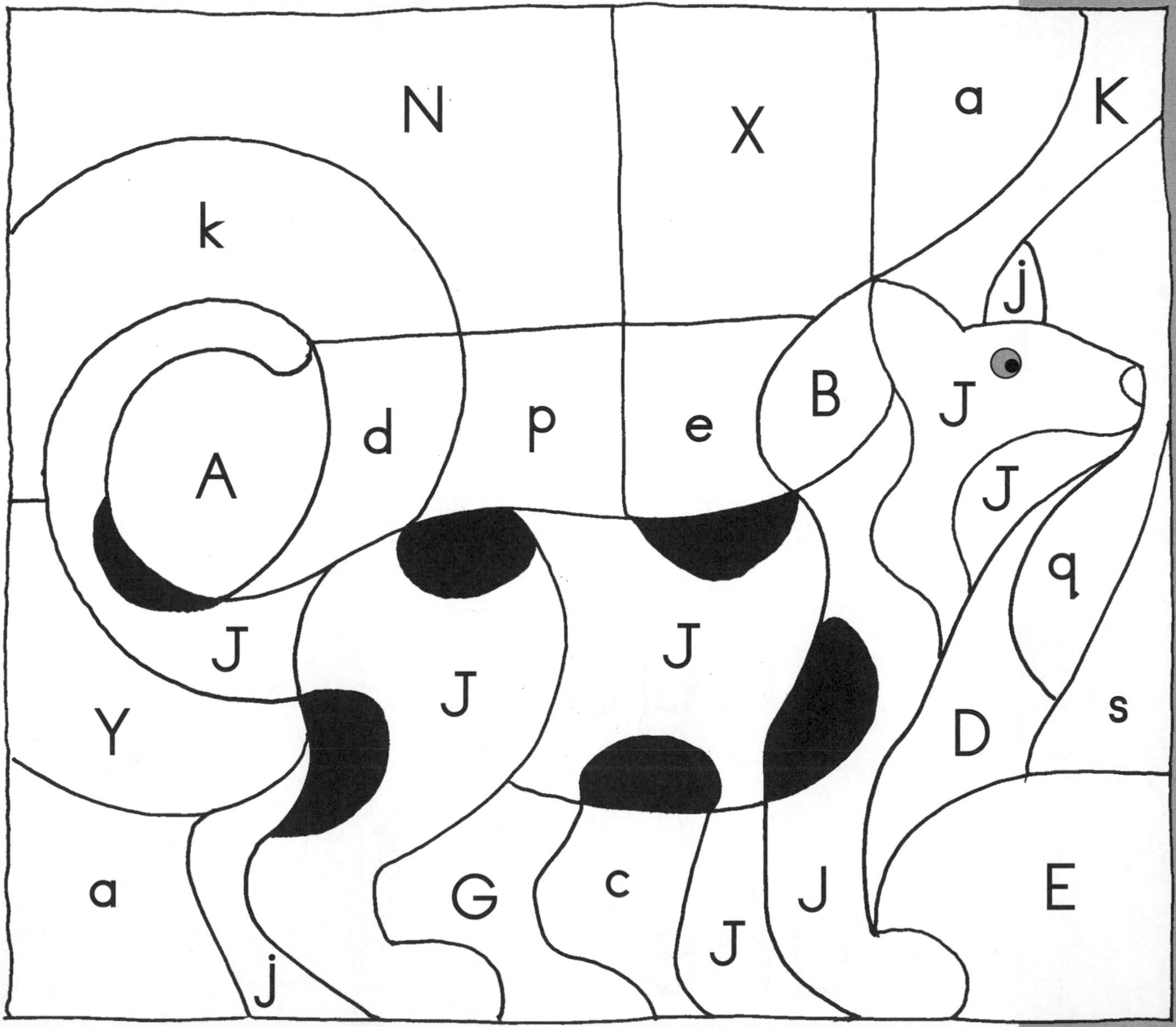

What animal do you see?

Jj

Trace the capital letter J.

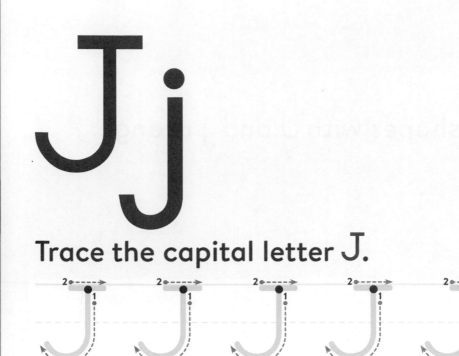

Now write the capital letter J.

Trace the J to complete each word.

Jaguar

June

Jacob

The **jaguar** loves to **jump** rope!

Trace the lowercase letter j.

j j j j j j j

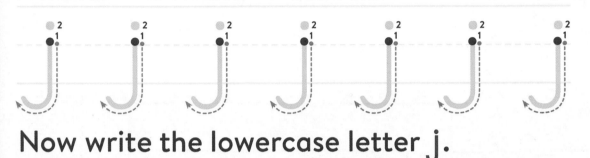

Now write the lowercase letter j.

Trace the j to complete each word.

jump

junior

major

Fun with K

Help the **kitten** find the **kite**!

Circle the letters K and k.

Then connect the circles.

What is the boy flying?

K k

Trace the capital letter K.

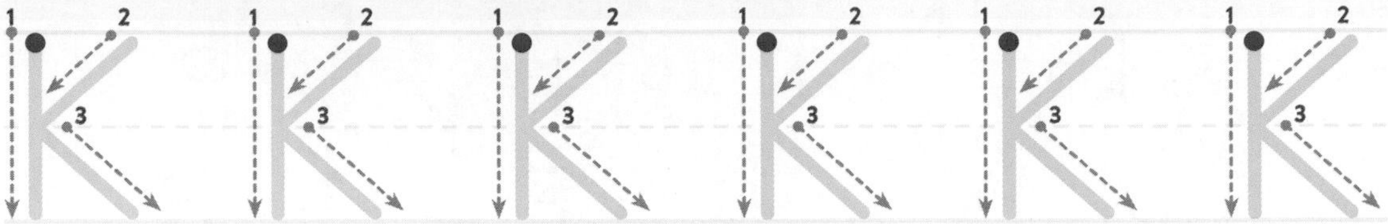

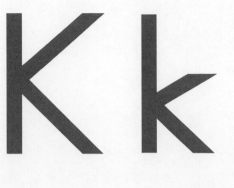

Now write the capital letter K.

Trace the K to complete each word.

Kitten

Kamil

Kate

The **kitten** flies her **kite**.

Trace the lowercase letter k.

k k k k k k k

Now write the lowercase letter k.

Trace the k to complete each word.

kite

kitchen

skin

Fun with L

Help the **lizard** find the **lion**!

Color the spaces with L light brown.
Color the spaces with l dark brown.

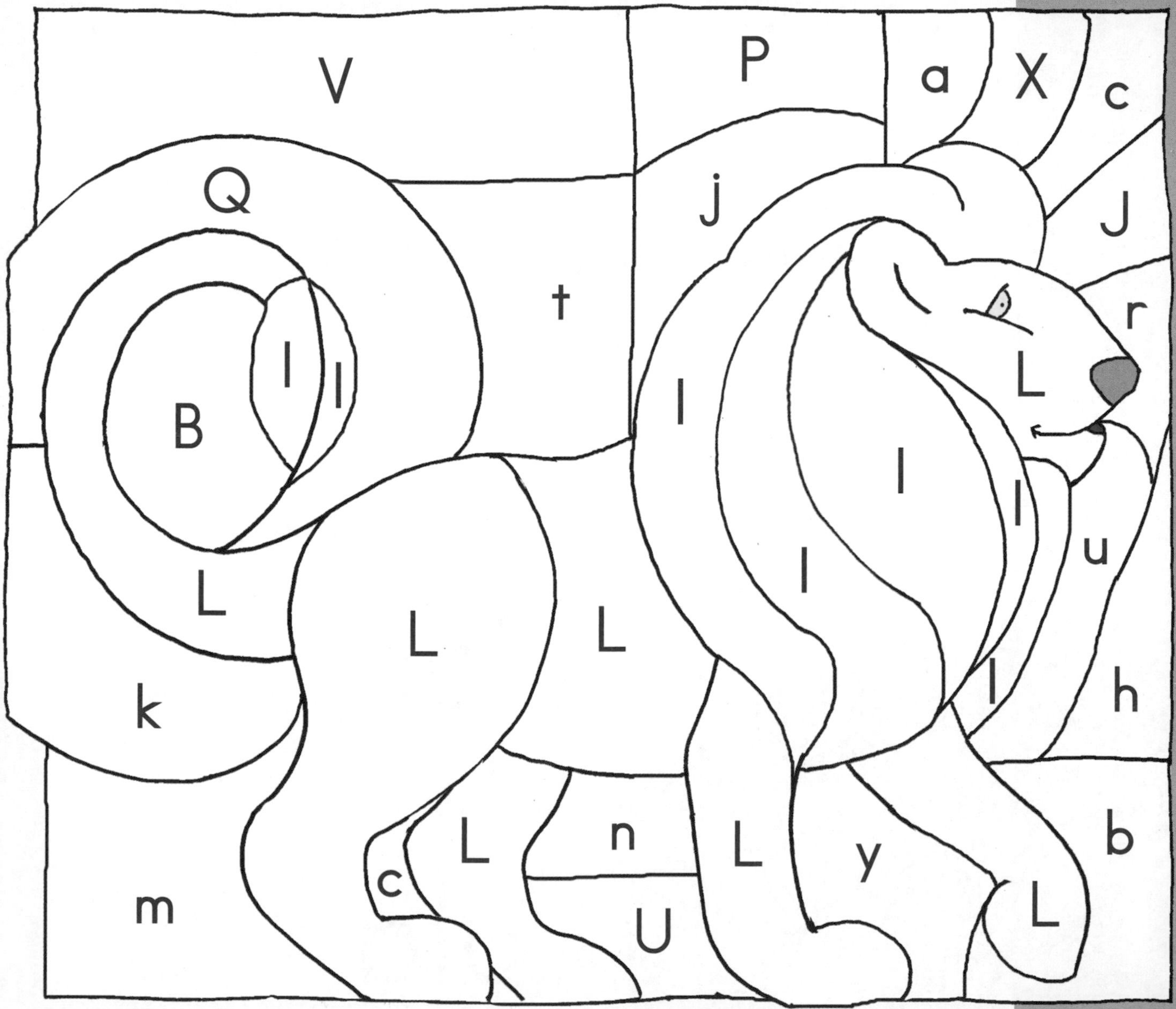

What animal do you see?

L l

Trace the capital letter L.

1 2 L L L L L L

Now write the capital letter L.

Trace the L to complete each word.

Lion

Lola

Lemon

Hooray! The **lion** is dancing with the **lizard**.

Trace the lowercase letter l.

Now write the lowercase letter l.

Trace the l to complete each word.

lake

leaf

plane

Fun with M

Help the **mermaid** swim to the **moon**!

Color the spaces with M and m yellow.

Color all the other spaces dark blue.

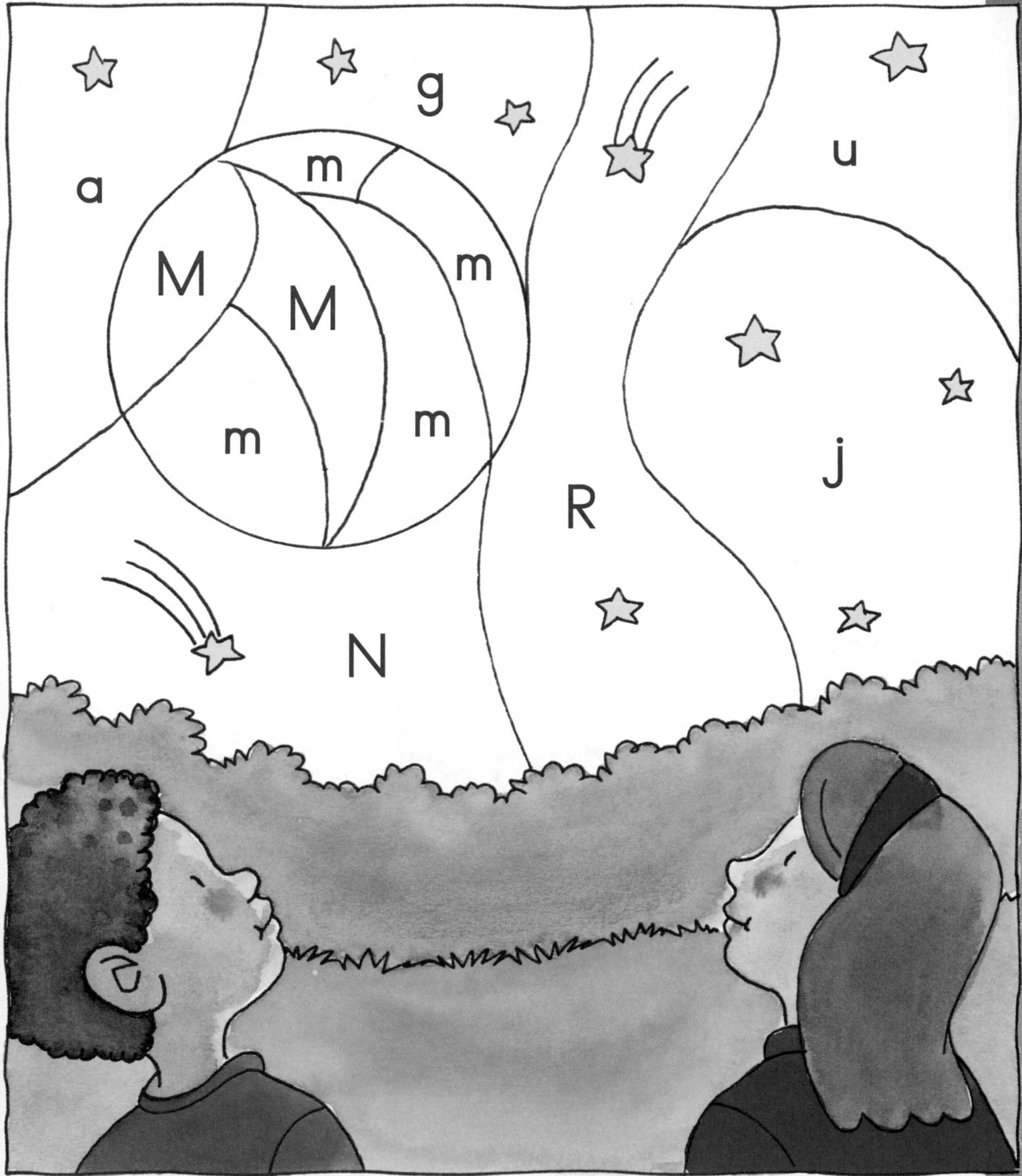

What do you see in the sky?

M m

Trace the capital letter M.

M M M M M

Now write the capital letter M.

Trace the M to complete each word.

Mermaid

Maria

Mom

All the **mermaids** want to go to the **moon**!

Trace the lowercase letter m.

m m m m m m

Now write the lowercase letter m.

Trace the m to complete each word.

moon

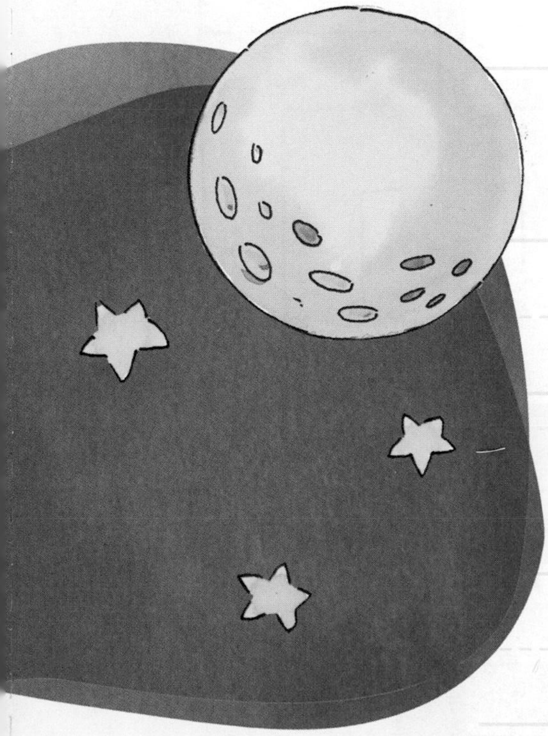

hammer

smile

Fun with N

Help the **nightingale** find the **nest**!

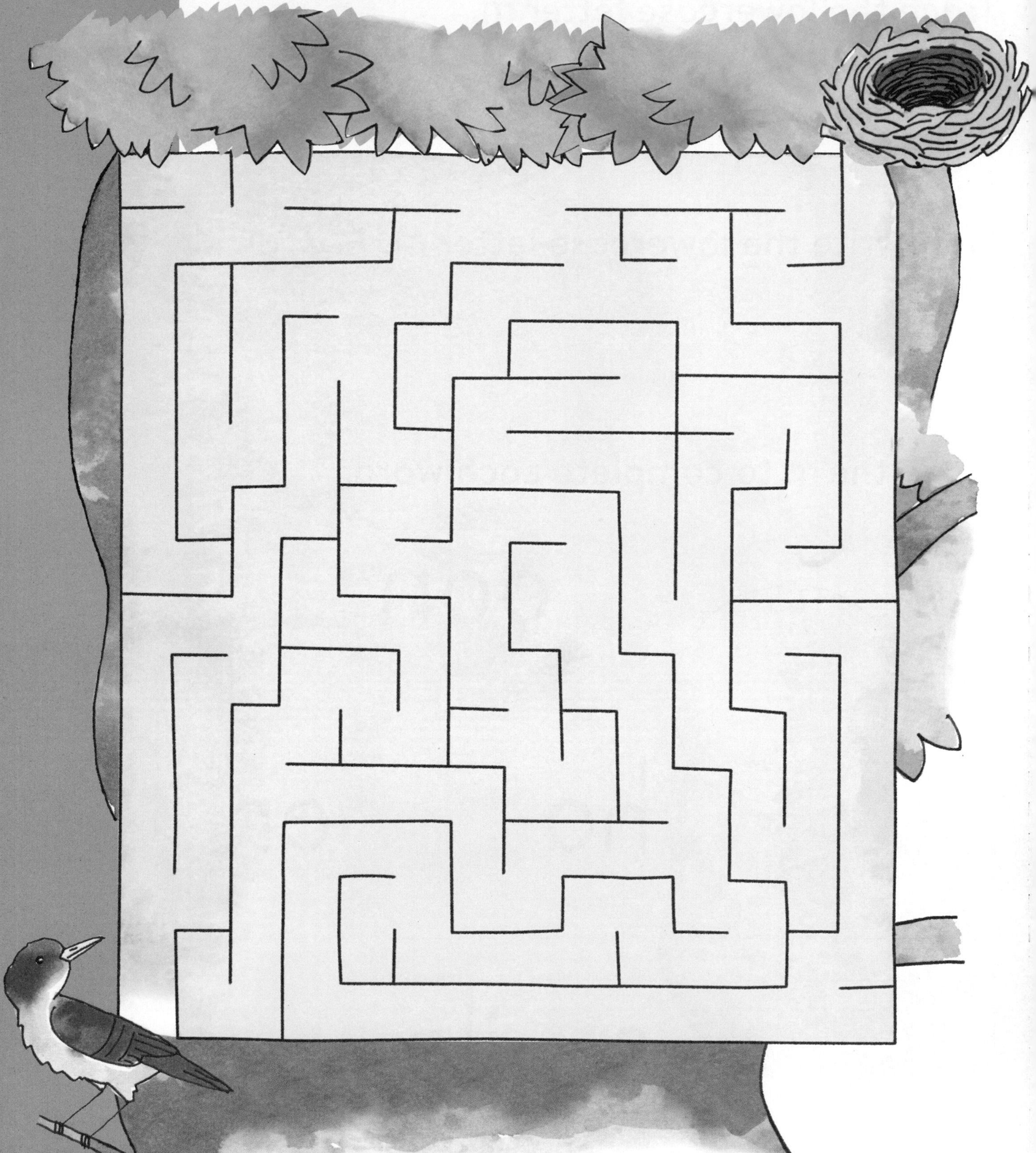

Color the spaces with N dark brown.

Color the spaces with n light brown.

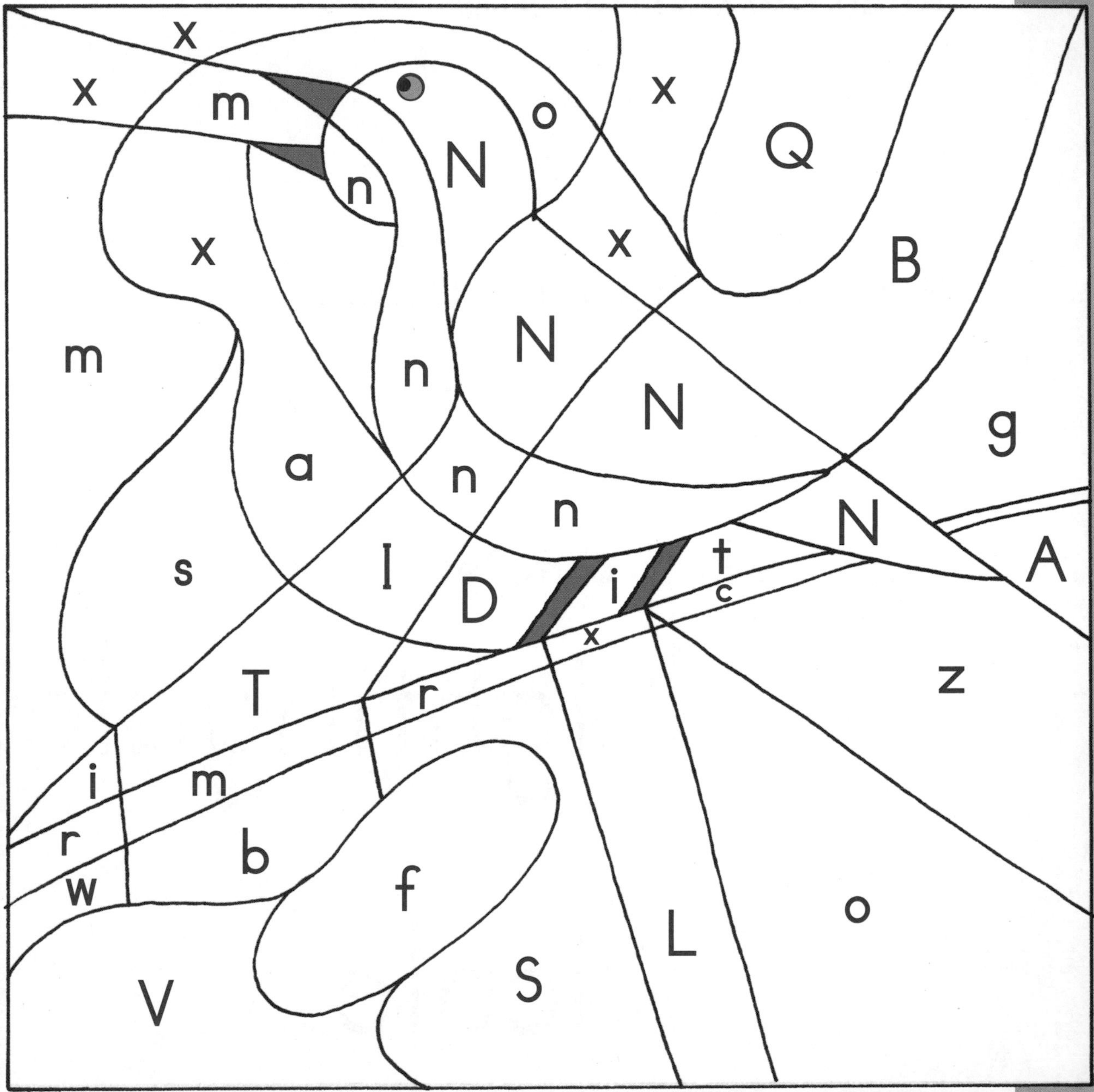

What animal do you see?

N n

Trace the capital letter N.

1 2 N 3 1 2 N 3 1 2 N 3 1 2 N 3 1 2 N 3 1 2 N 3

Now write the capital letter N.

Trace the N to complete each word.

Nightingale

Nicole

Now

The **nightingale** wants to rest in the **nest**!

Trace the lowercase letter n.

n n n n n n n

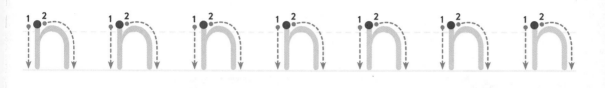

Now write the lowercase letter n.

Trace the n to complete each word.

nest

barn

not

Fun with O

Help the **otter** find the **octopus**!

Color the spaces with O pink.
Color the spaces with o red.

What animal do you see?

O o

Trace the capital letter O.

O O O O O O

Now write the capital letter O.

Trace the O to complete each word.

Octopus

Ox

Oliver

The **octopus** wants to swim with the **otter**!

Trace the lowercase letter o.

1 o 1 o 1 o 1 o 1 o 1 o 1 o

Now write the lowercase letter o.

Trace the o to complete each word.

otter

box

hot

Fun with P

Look at all the **penguins**!

Circle the four animals that should not be in this penguin **parade.**

Color all the circles with P and p red.

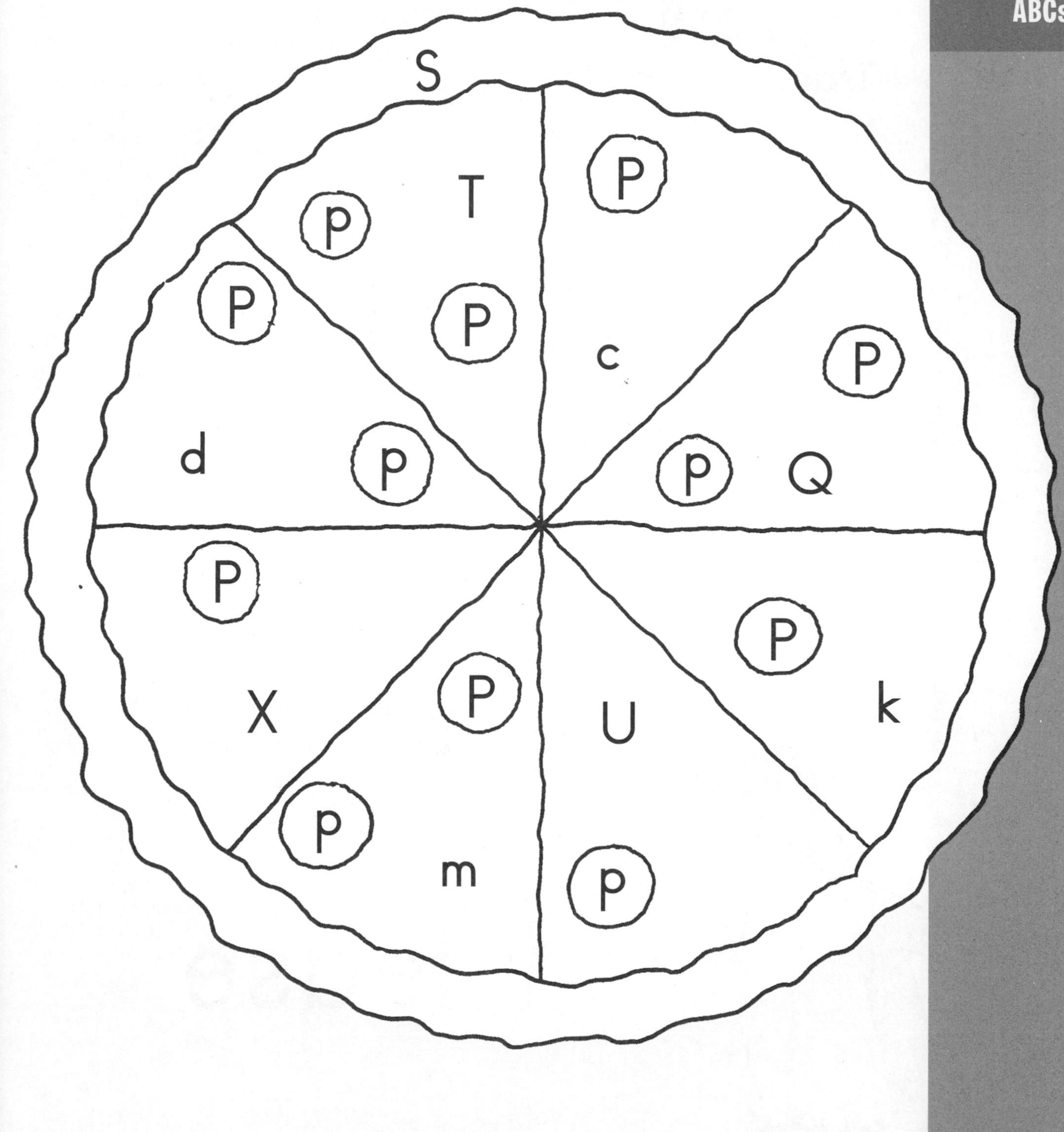

What kind of pizza did you make?

P p

Trace the capital letter P.

P P P P P P

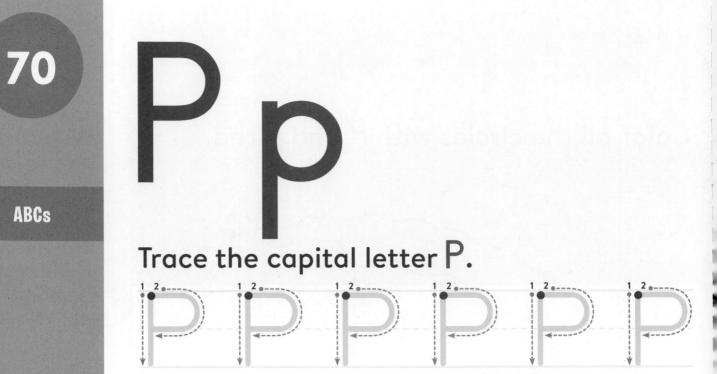

Now write the capital letter P.

Trace the P to complete each word.

Penguin

Please

Pablo

The **penguin** is hungry for **pizza**!

Trace the lowercase letter p.

p p p p p p p

Now write the lowercase letter p.

Trace the p to complete each word.

pizza

pumpkin

pot

Fun with Q

Help the **queen** find her **quill.**

Color the spaces with Q and q yellow.

Color all the other spaces different colors.

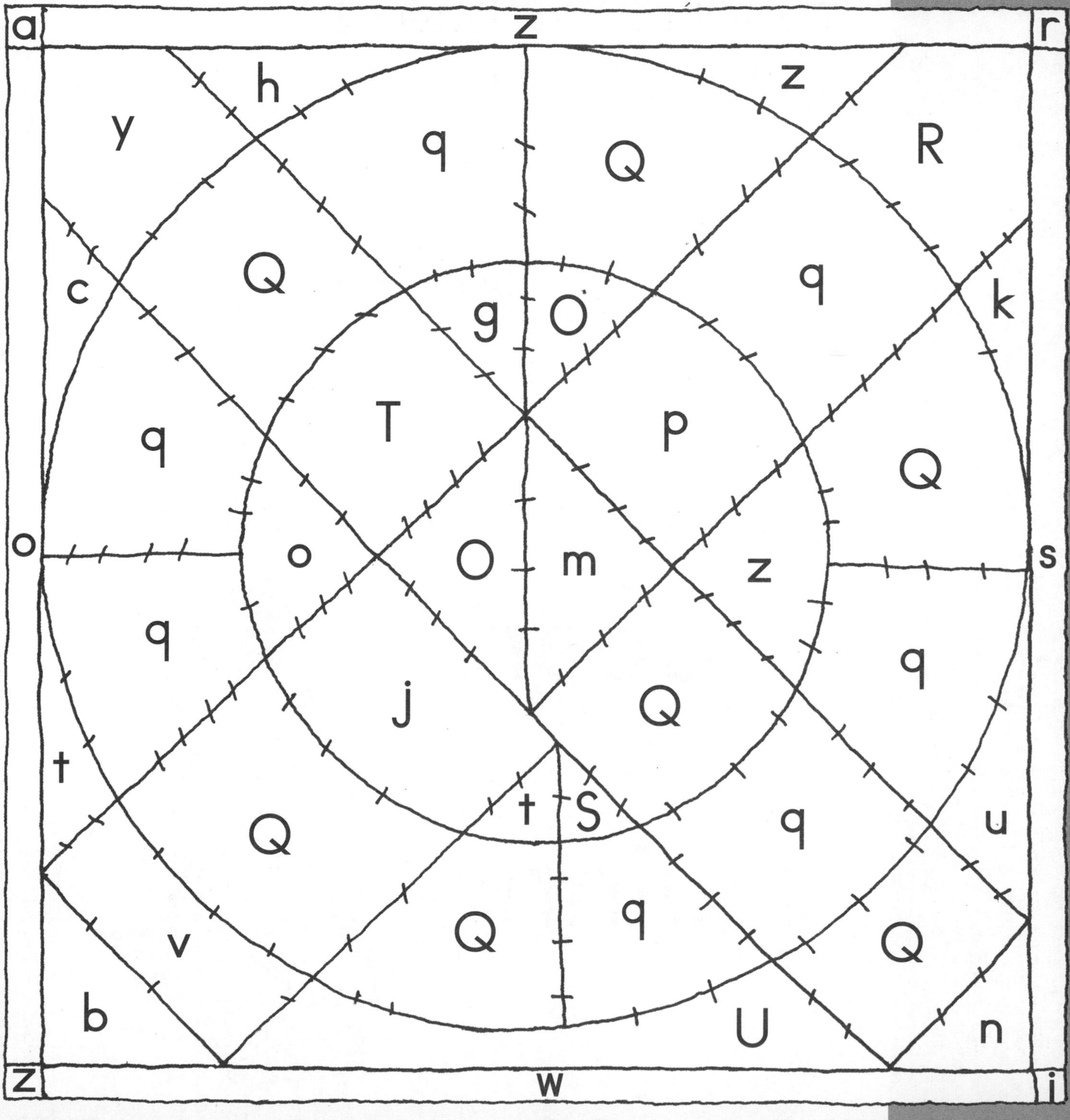

What letter do you see?

Q q

Trace the capital letter Q.

Q Q Q Q Q Q

Now write the capital letter Q.

Trace the Q to complete each word.

Queen

Quinn

Quiet

The **queen** is patching her **quilt**.

Trace the lowercase letter q.

q q q q q q

Now write the lowercase letter q.

Trace the q to complete each word.

quilt

quote

equal

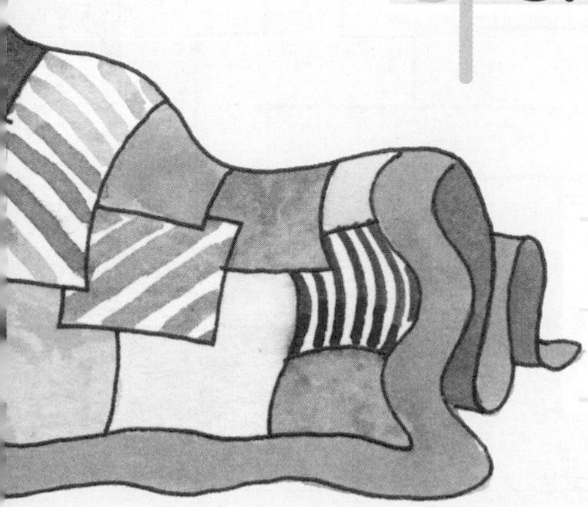

Fun with R

Help the **rabbit** cross the **river**!

Color the spaces with R and r gray.

What animal do you see?

Rr

Trace the capital letter R.

R R R R R R

Now write the capital letter R.

Trace the R to complete each word.

Rabbit

Rosa

Rocks

The **raccoon** wants to play with the **rabbit**!

Trace the lowercase letter r.

r r r r r r r

Now write the lowercase letter r.

Trace the r to complete each word.

river

run

bird

Fun with S

Help the **spaceship** get to the **star**!

Color the spaces with S and s gray.

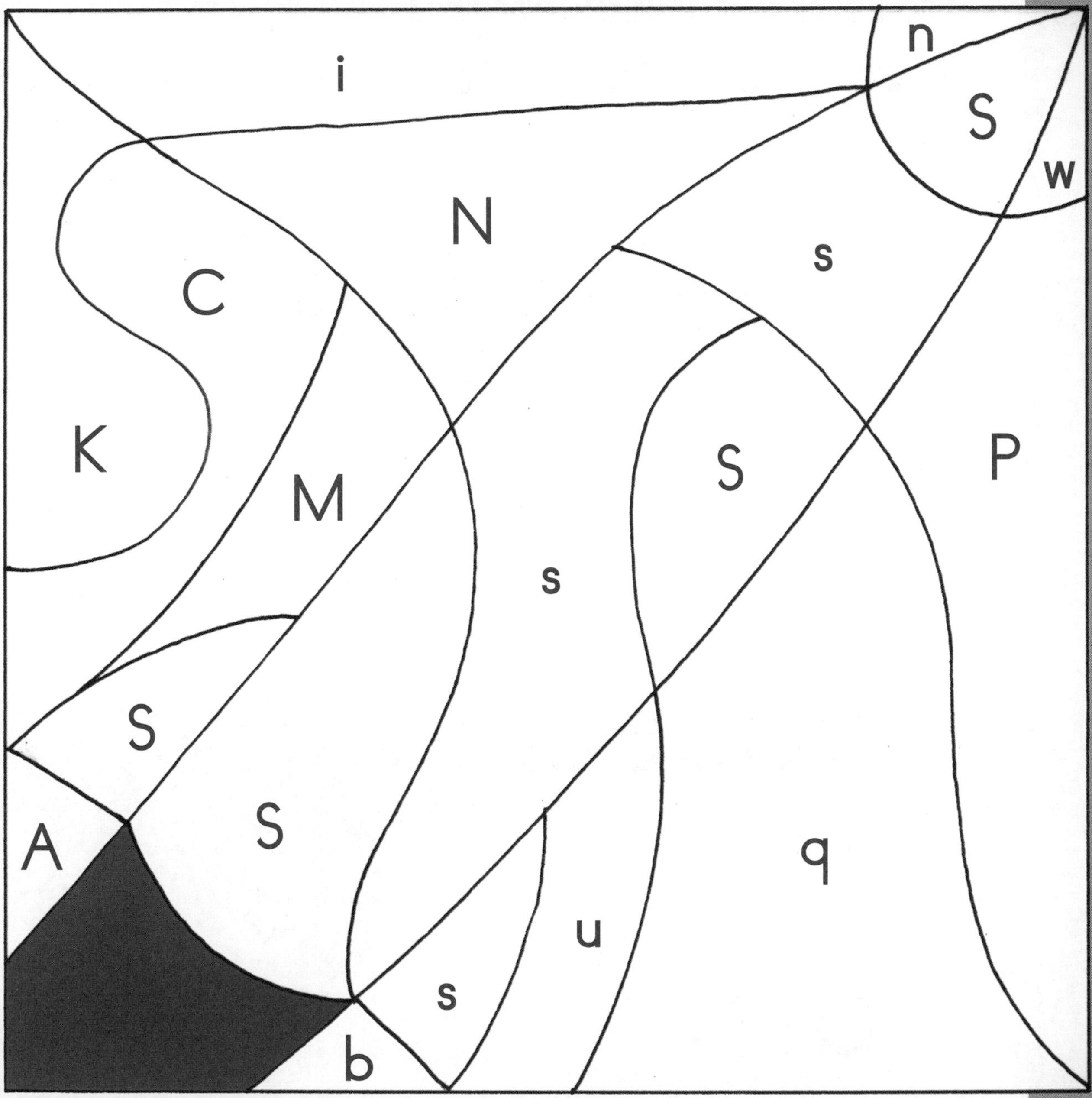

What do you see?

S s

Trace the capital letter S.

S S S S S S S

Now write the capital letter S.

Trace the S to complete each word.

Spaceship

Sam

Soup

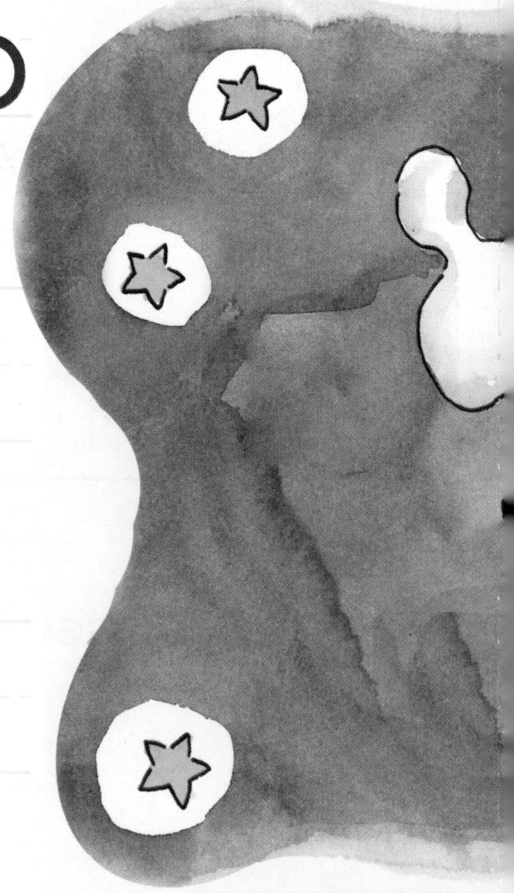

The **spaceship** is soaring past the **stars**!

Trace the lowercase letter **s**.

s s s s s s s

Now write the lowercase letter **s**.

Trace the **s** to complete each word.

stars

pass

slide

Fun with T

Help the **toucan** get to its nest in the **tree**!

Color the spaces with T black.

Color the spaces with t yellow.

What animal do you see?

T t

Trace the capital letter T.

T T T T T T T

Now write the capital letter T.

Trace the T to complete each word.

Tomato

Table

Tuesday

All the **toucans** want to sit in the **tree**!

Trace the lowercase letter t.

Now write the lowercase letter t.

Trace the t to complete each word.

bats

write

acrobat

Fun with U

What animal is hiding in the grass?

To find out, connect the dots from 1 to 12.

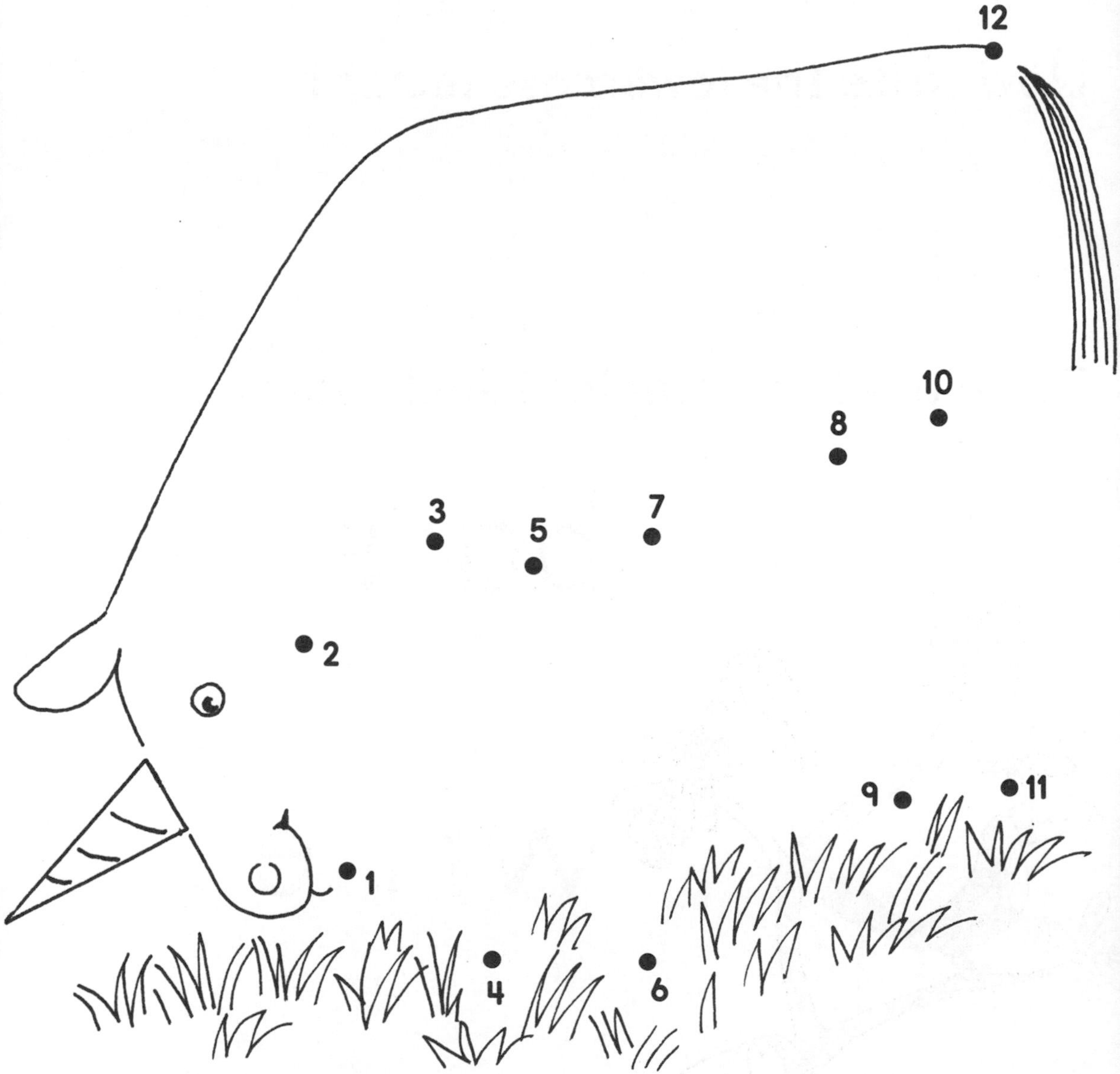

What do you need in the rain?

Draw a line down the path with U and u.

U u

Trace the capital letter U.

U U U U U U

Now write the capital letter U.

Trace the U to complete each word.

Unicorn

Uncle

Under

The **unicorn** needs an **umbrella**!

Trace the lowercase letter u.

u u u u u u u

Now write the lowercase letter u.

Trace the u to complete each word.

umbrella

sunny

bush

Fun with V

Help the **vulture** find the **violin**!

Color the spaces with V black.

Color the spaces with v gray.

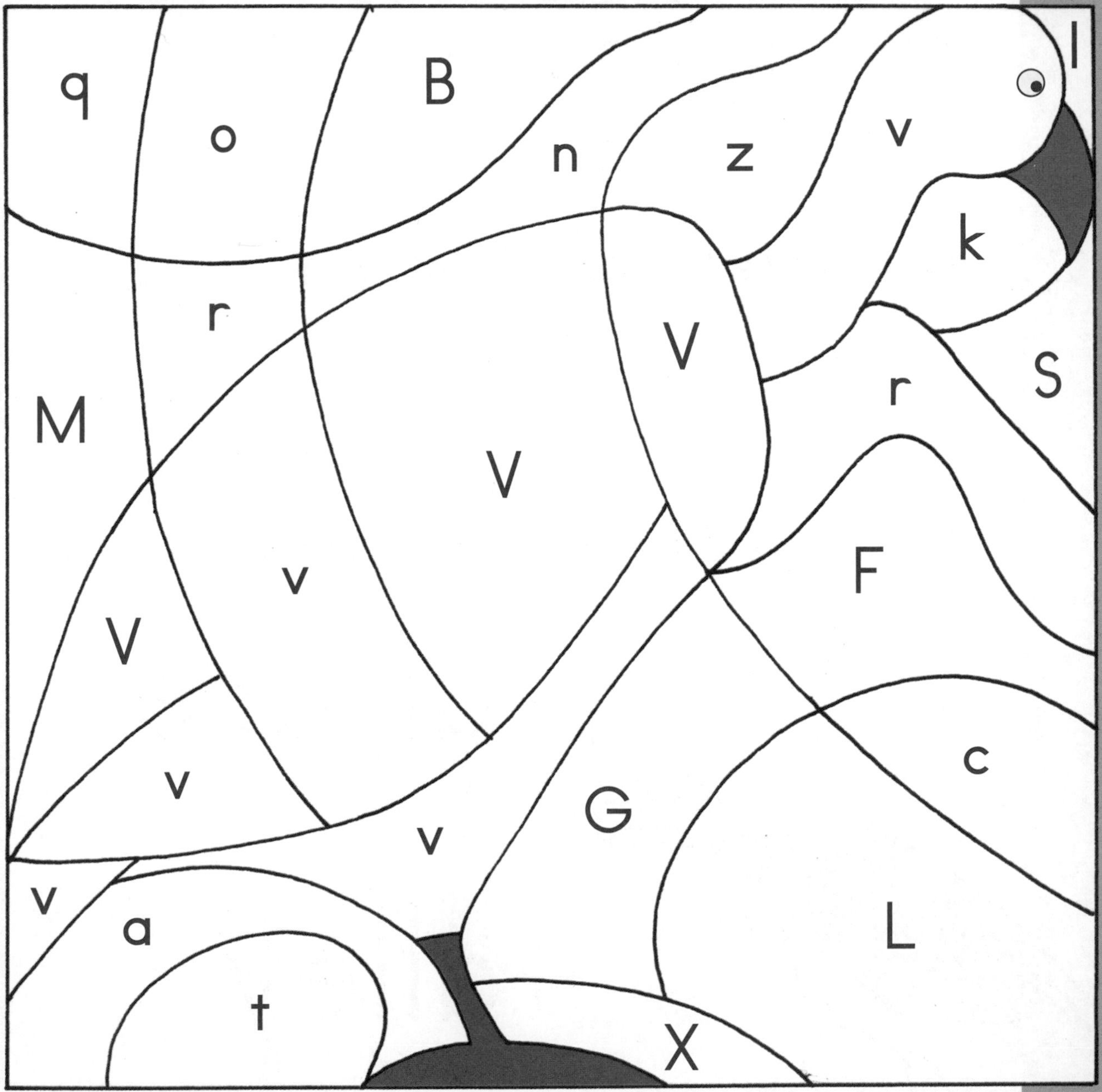

What animal do you see?

V v

Trace the capital letter V.

V V V V V V

Now write the capital letter V.

Trace the V to complete each word.

Vulture

Valley

Vermont

The **vulture** loves to listen to the **violin**!

Trace the lowercase letter v.

v v v v v v v

Now write the lowercase letter v.

Trace the v to complete each word.

violin

vase

never

Fun with W

Help the **wizard** find the **whale**!

Color the spaces with W yellow.

Color the spaces with **w** blue.

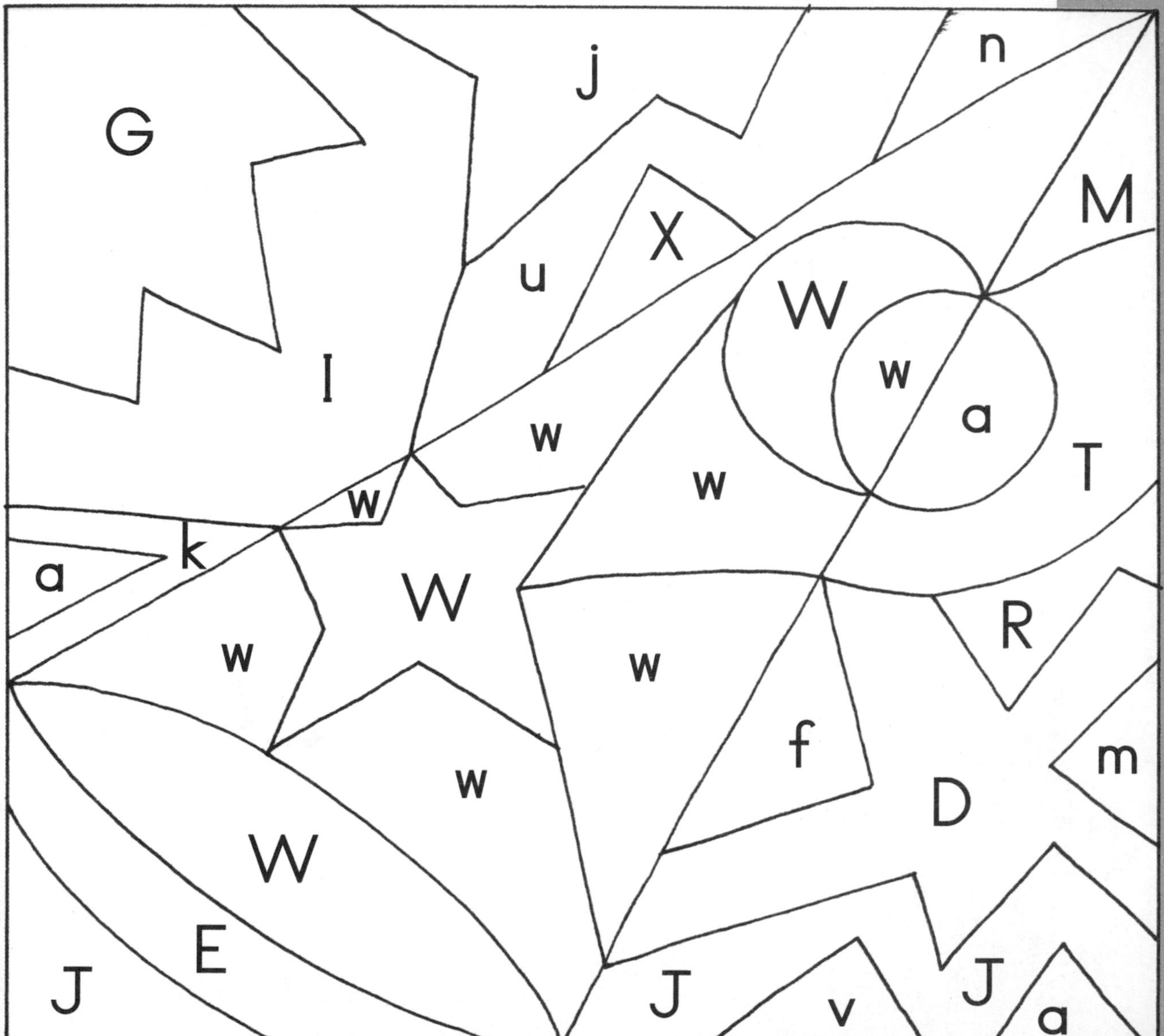

What do you see?

W w

Trace the capital letter W.

W W W W

Now write the capital letter W.

Trace the W to complete each word.

Wizard

Will

World

The **wizard** casts a spell on the **whale**!

Trace the lowercase letter w.

w w w w w

Now write the lowercase letter w.

Trace the w to complete each word.

whale

wave

cow

Fun with X

Help the snake find his **X-ray**!

Help the pirate find the treasure.

Draw a line up the path with X and x.

X x

Trace the capital letter X.

1 2 X 1 2 X 1 2 X 1 2 X 1 2 X 1 2 X

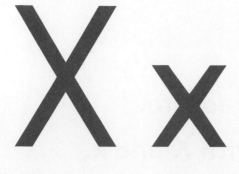

Now write the capital letter X.

Trace the X to complete each word.

X-ray

Xavier

Xylophone

The X-ray machine is working!

Trace the lowercase letter x.

x x x x x x x

Now write the lowercase letter x.

Trace the x to complete each word.

box

taxi

exact

Fun with Y

Help the **yak** find the **yarn**.

Color the spaces with Y dark brown.

Color the spaces with y light brown.

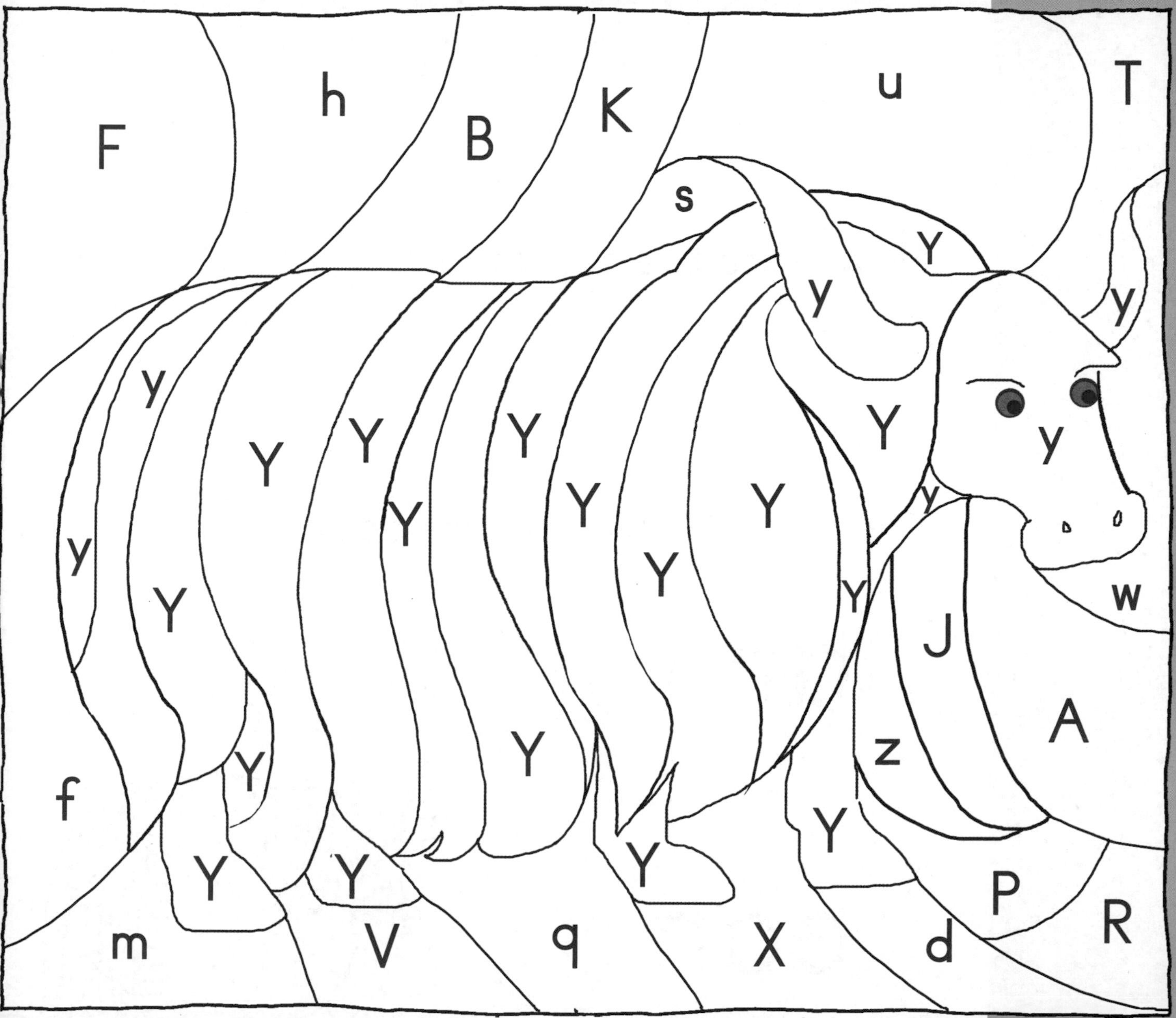

What animal do you see?

Yy

Trace the capital letter Y.

Y Y Y Y Y Y

Now write the capital letter Y.

Trace the Y to complete each word.

Yarn

Year

Yoshi

The **yak** is wearing a **yellow** sweater!

Trace the lowercase letter y.

y y y y y y y

Now write the lowercase letter y.

Trace the y to complete each word.

yellow

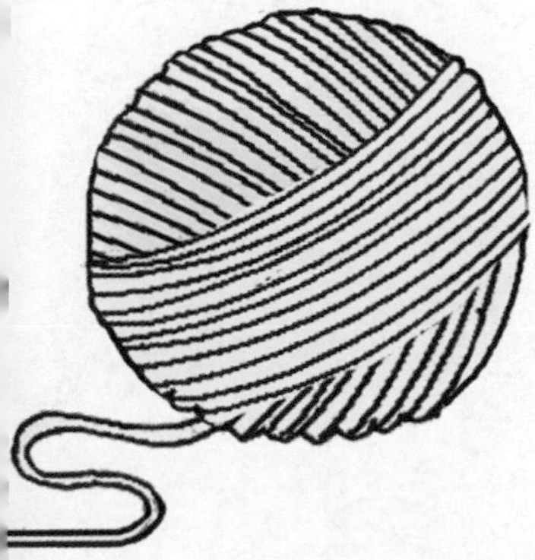

silly

yard

Fun with Z

Help the baby **zebra** find his mother!

Color the spaces with Z and z red.

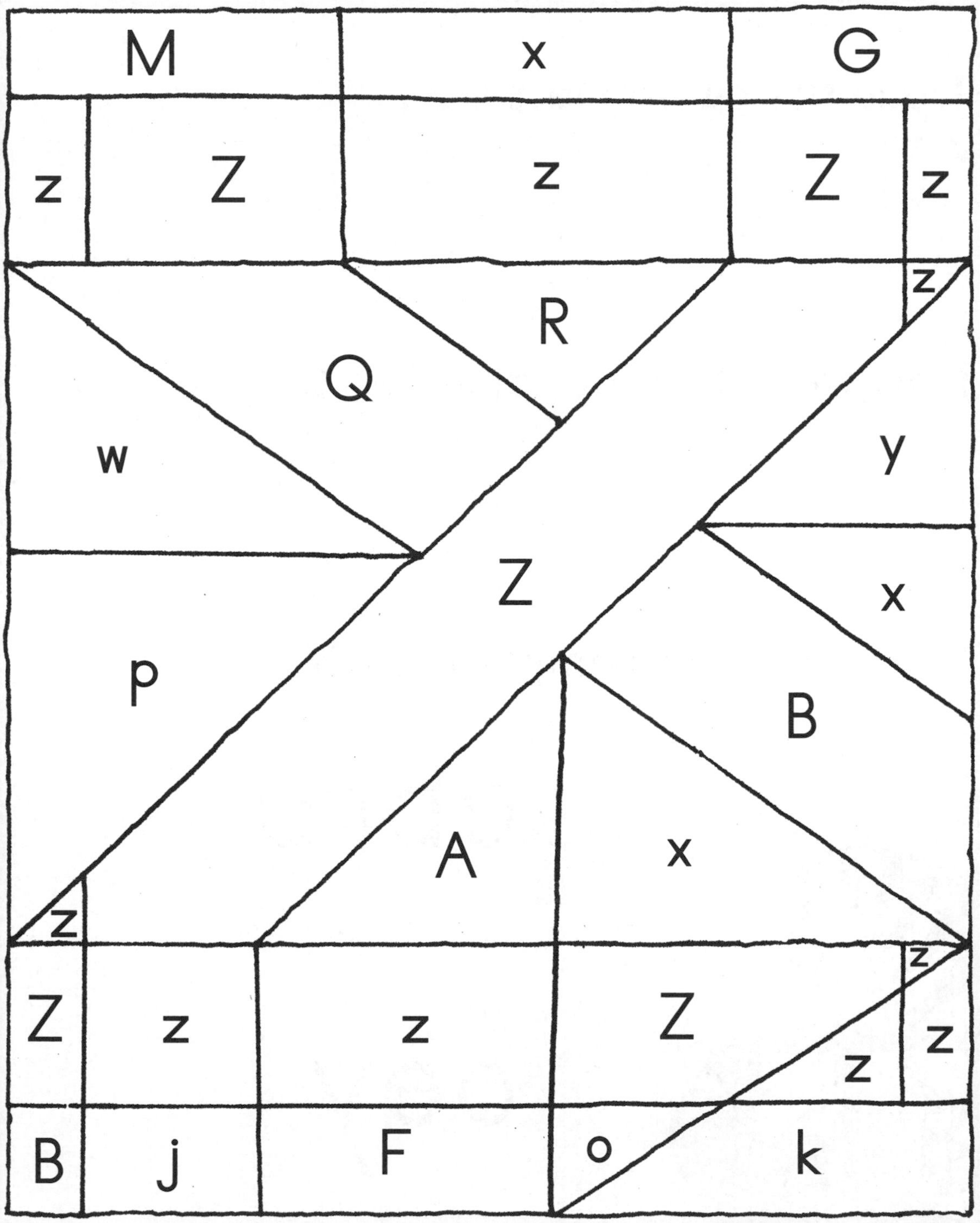

What letter do you see?

Z z

Trace the capital letter Z.

Z Z Z Z Z Z

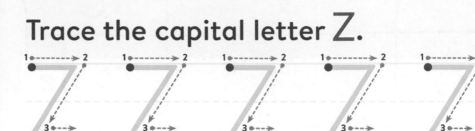

Now write the capital letter Z.

Trace the Z to complete each word.

Zebra

Zoey

Zero

The **zebra** is in the **zoo**!

Trace the lowercase letter z.

z z z z z z z

Now write the lowercase letter z.

Trace the z to complete each word.

zoo

lizard

lazy

Hat Trick!

Help the monster find his hat!
Connect the dots from A to M.

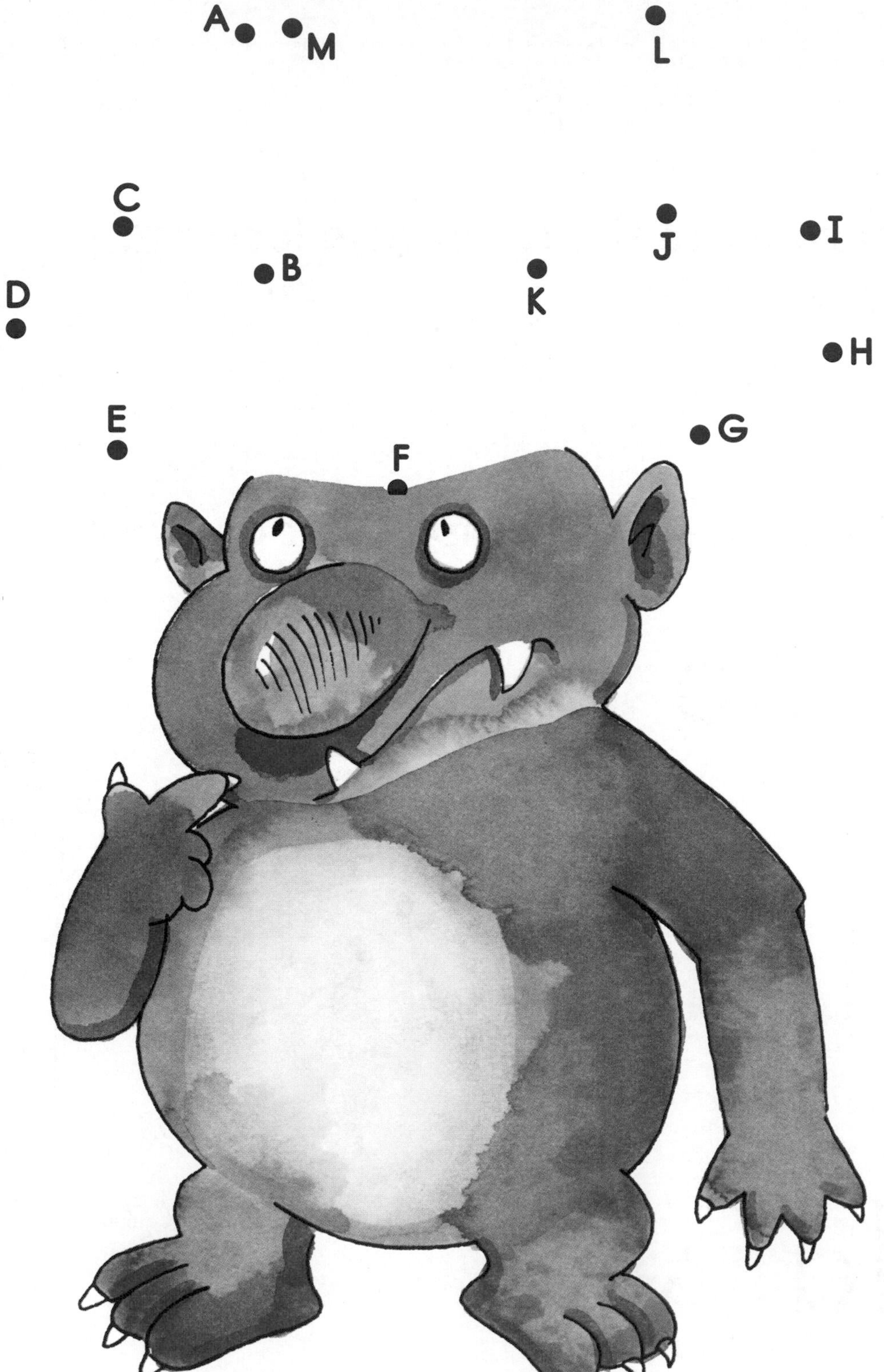

Move It!

Help this girl get around!
Connect the letters in A–B–C order.
Start with the letter N.

Name Game

What letters are in your first name?

Circle the first letter of your first name.

A B C D E F G H I

J K L M N O P Q R

S T U V W X Y Z

Circle the rest of the letters in your first name.

a b c d e f g h i

j k l m n o p q r

s t u v w x y z

Now write your name!

PHONICS

Look around the room—
say the name of the first
object you see. What sound does
it start with? End with?
Let's learn more about
letter sounds!

PARENTS Help prepare your child to read by playing with letter sounds and words. Point out words that rhyme, clap the syllables in your child's name, blend sounds to make a word, and stretch out words to hear individual sounds.

PLACE A STICKER HERE

A as in Apple

Apple begins with the A sound.

Say the word for each picture.

Circle the pictures that begin with the A sound.

B as in Bike

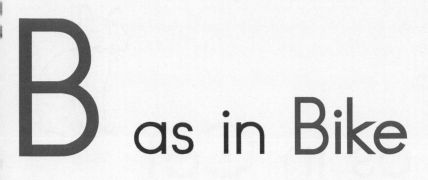

Bike begins with the B sound.

Say the word for each picture.

Circle the pictures that begin with the B sound.

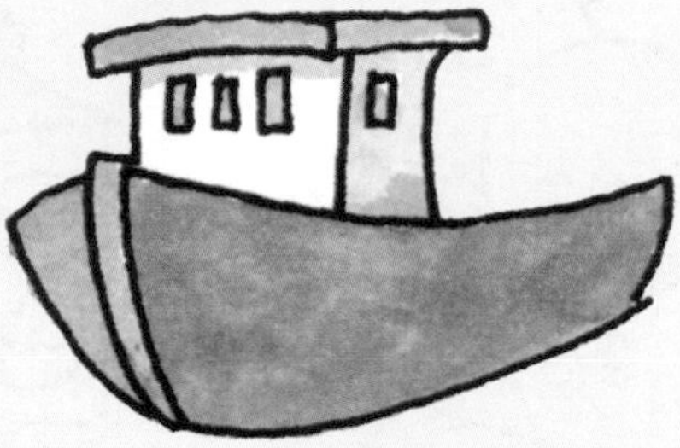

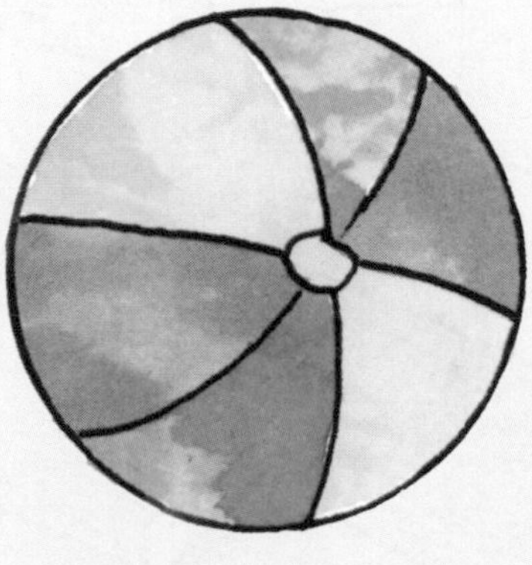

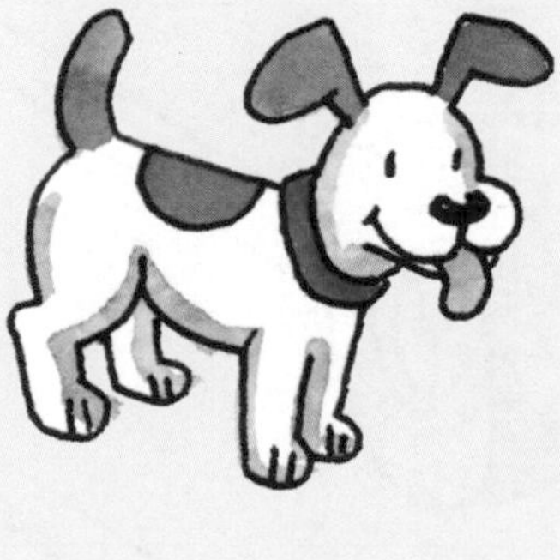

C as in Cat

Cat begins with the C sound.

Say the word for each thing in the picture.

Circle the things that begin with the C sound.

D as in Dog

Dog begins with the D sound.

Say the word for each thing in the picture.

Circle the things that begin with the D sound.

E as in Egg

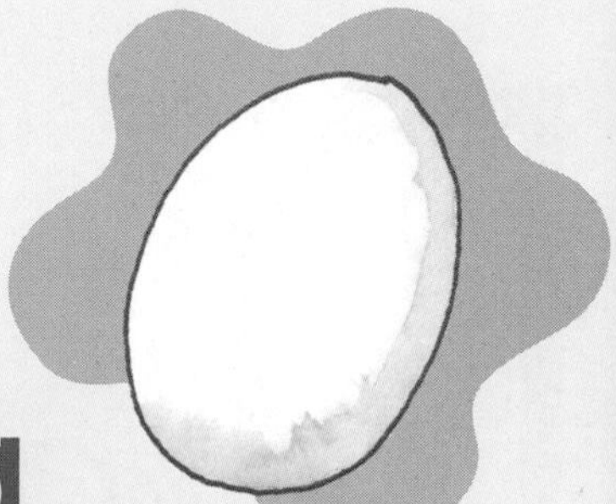

Egg begins with the E sound.

Say the word for each picture.

Circle the pictures that begin with the E sound.

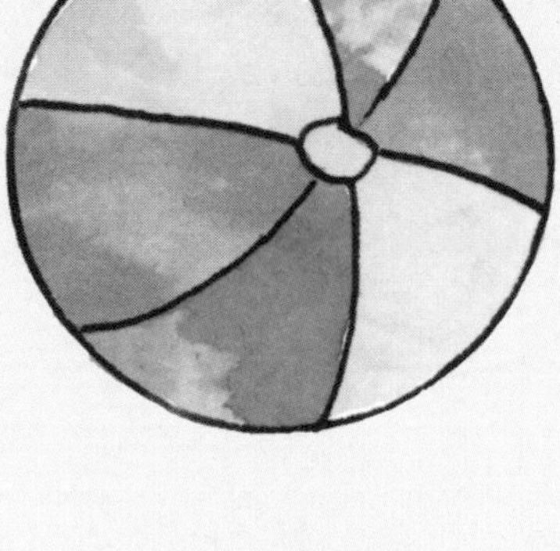

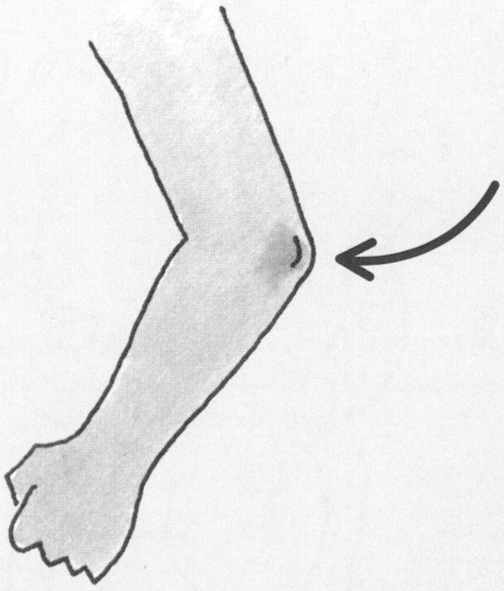

F as in Flag

Flag begins with the F sound.

Say the word for each picture.

Circle the pictures that begin with the F sound.

G as in Gate

Gate begins with the G sound.

Say the word for each thing in the picture.

Circle the things that begin with the G sound.

H as in House

House begins with the H sound. Say the word for the picture in each window.

Circle the pictures that begin with the H sound.

I as in Insect

Insect begins with the I sound.
Say the word for each picture.

Circle the pictures that begin with the I sound.

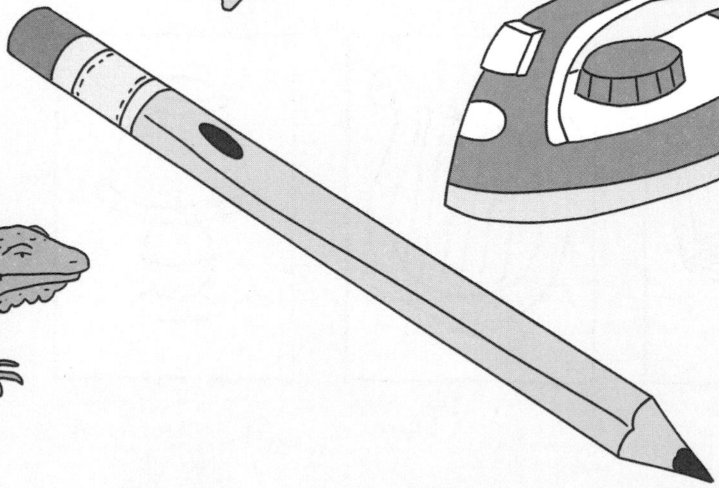

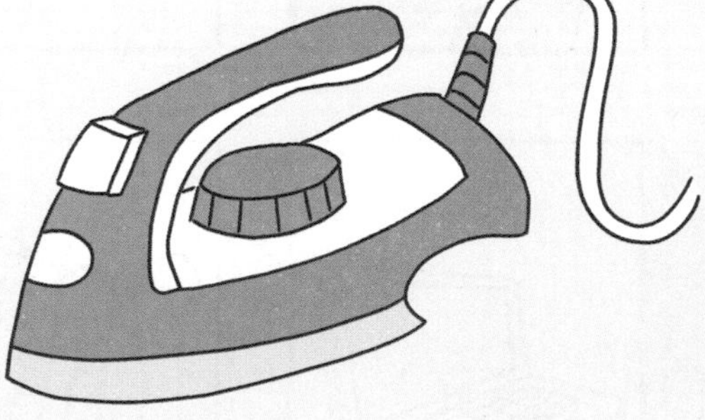

J as in Jelly

Jelly begins with the J sound. Say the word for each thing in the picture.

Circle the things that begin with the J sound.

K as in Key

Key begins with the K sound.

Say the word for the picture on each door.

Circle the pictures that begin with the K sound.

L as in Lizard

Lizard begins with the L sound.

Say the word for each picture.

Circle the pictures that begin with the L sound.

M as in Mouse

Mouse begins with the M sound.

Say the word for each thing in the picture.

Circle the things that begin with the M sound.

N as in Nose

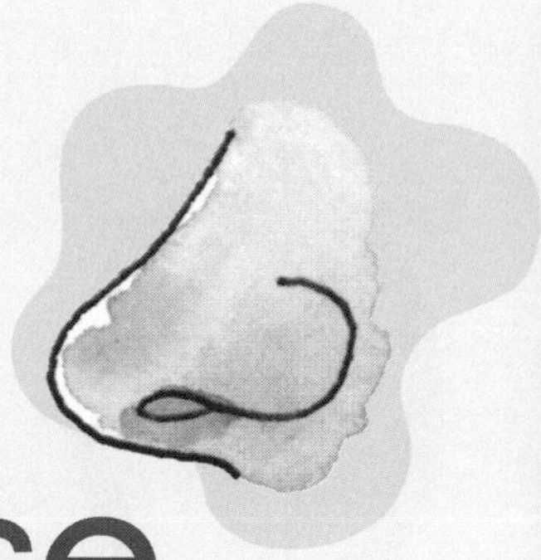

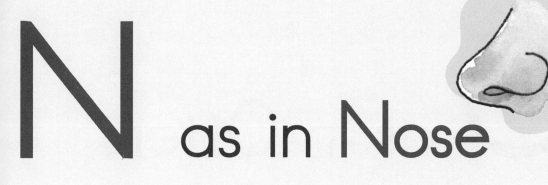

Nose begins with the N sound.

Say the word for each picture.

Circle the pictures that begin with the N sound.

O as in Otter

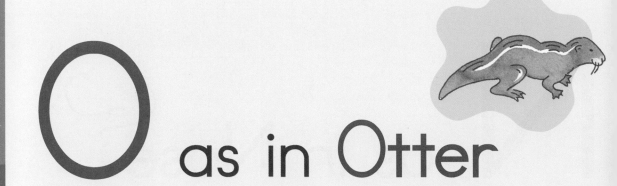

Otter begins with the O sound.

Say the word for each picture.

Circle the pictures that begin with the O sound.

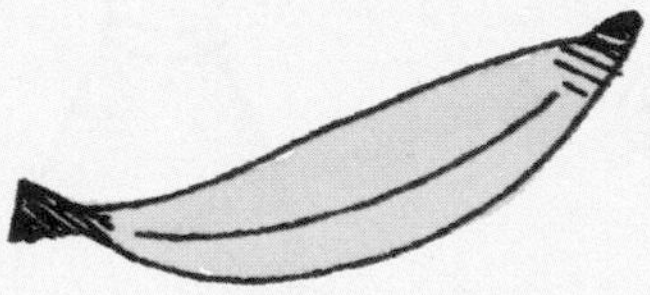

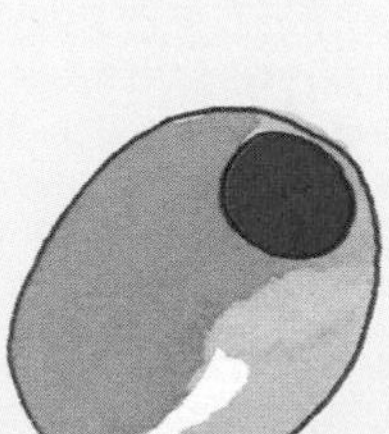

P as in Pirate

Pirate begins with the P sound.

Say the word for each thing in the picture.

Circle the things in the picture that begin with the P sound.

Q as in Queen

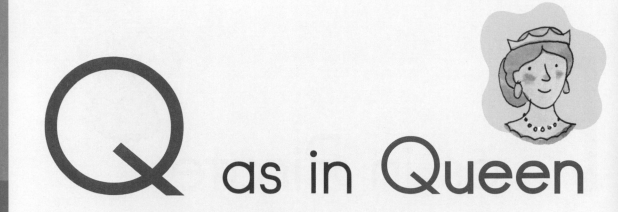

Queen begins with the Q sound.

Say the word for each thing in the picture.

Circle the things that begin with the Q sound.

R as in Raccoon

Raccoon begins with the R sound.

Say the word for each thing in the picture.

Circle the things that begin with the R sound.

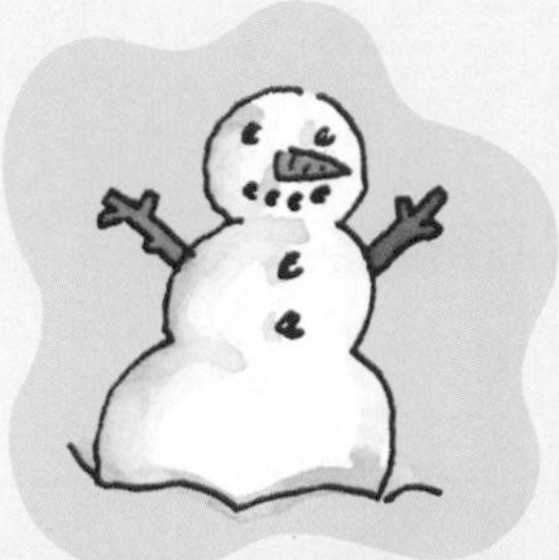

S as in Snowman

Snowman begins with the S sound.

Say the word for each picture.

Circle the pictures that begin with the S sound.

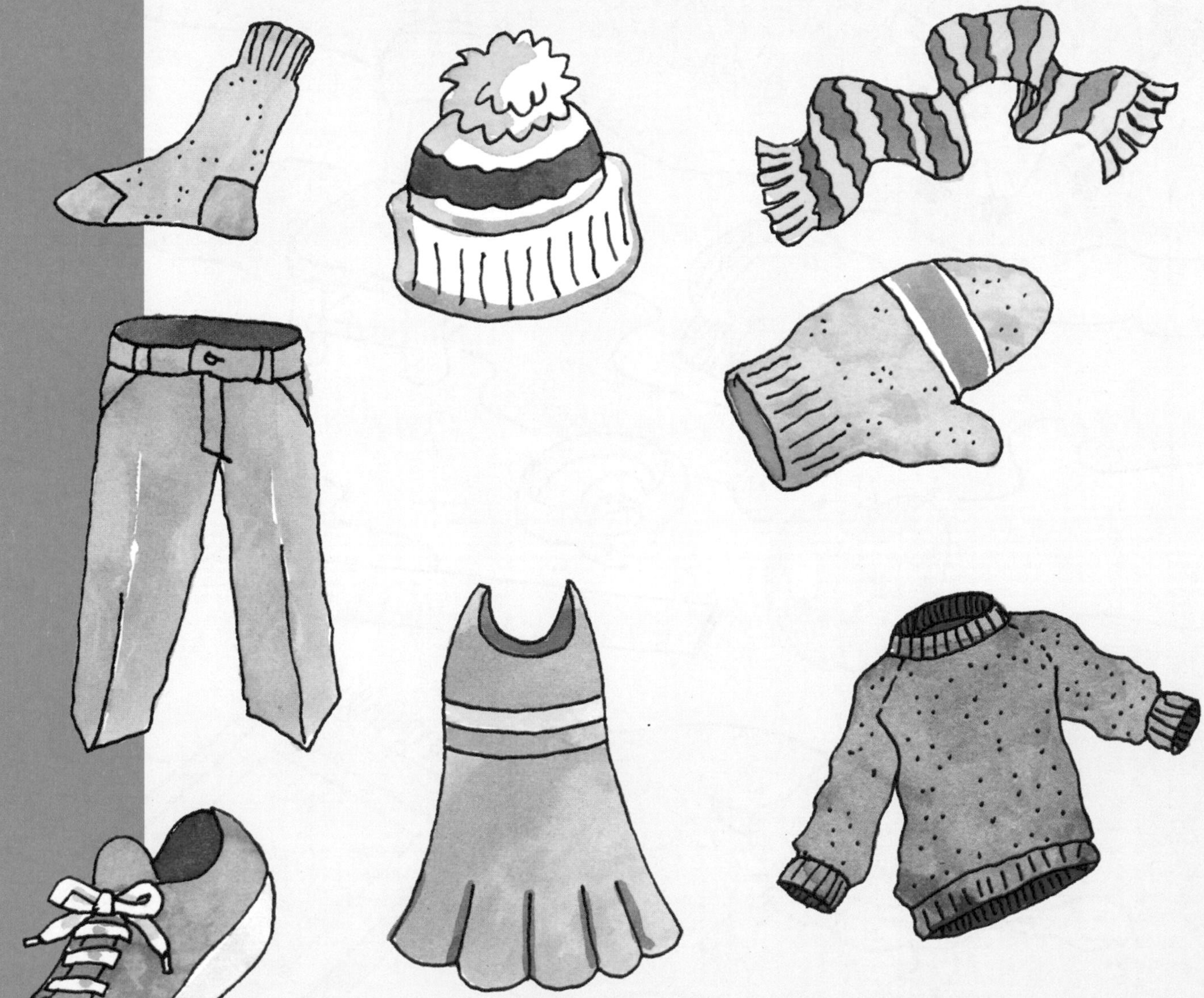

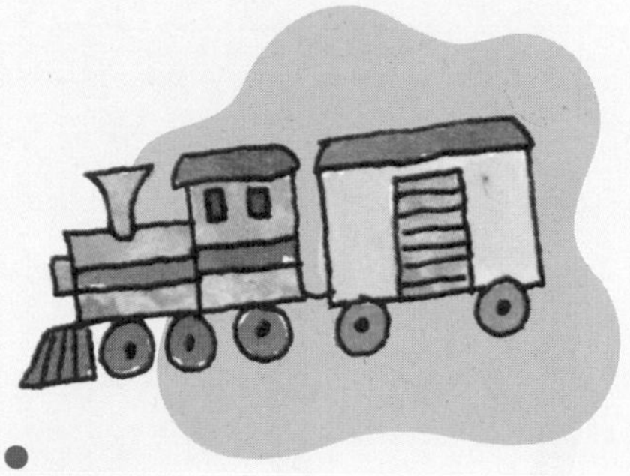

T as in Train

Train begins with the T sound.

Say the word for each picture.

Circle the pictures that begin with the T sound.

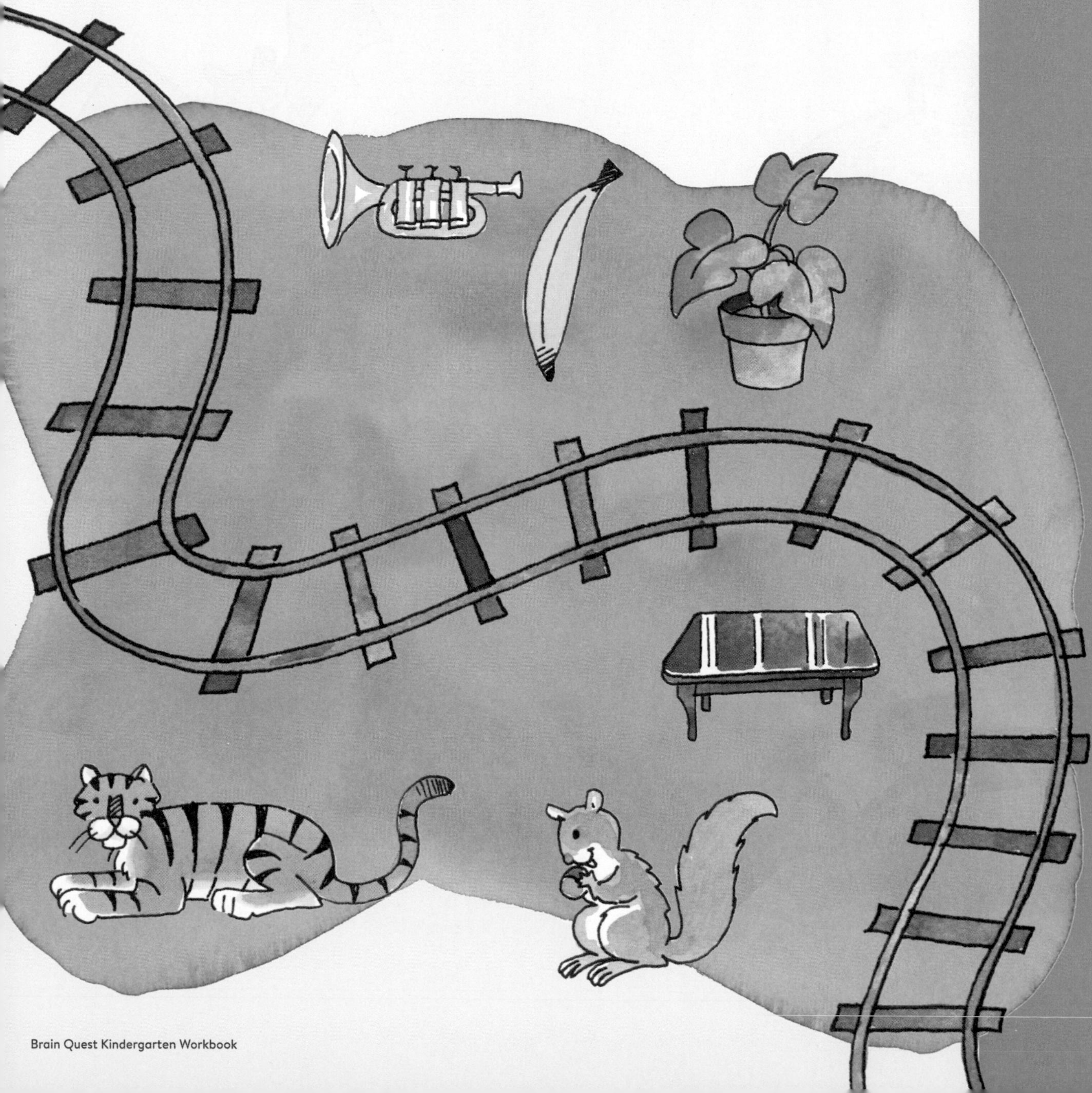

U as in Up

Up begins with the U sound.

Say the word for each picture.

Circle the pictures that begin with the U sound.

V as in Vine

Vine begins with the V sound.

Say the word for each thing on the vine.

Circle the things that begin with the V sound.

W as in Web

Web begins with the W sound.

Say the word for each thing in the web.

Circle the things that begin with the W sound.

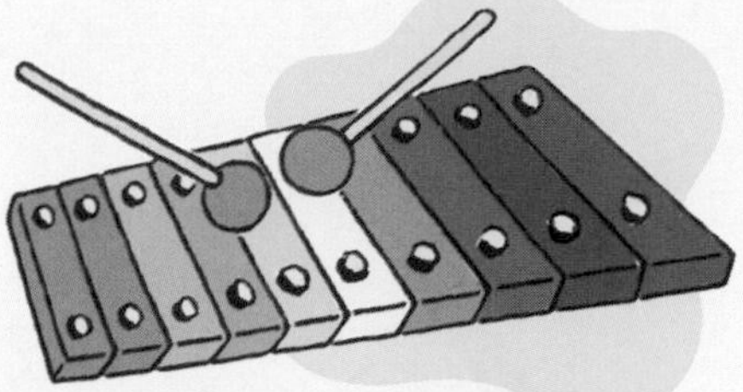

X as in Xylophone
Y as in Yellow

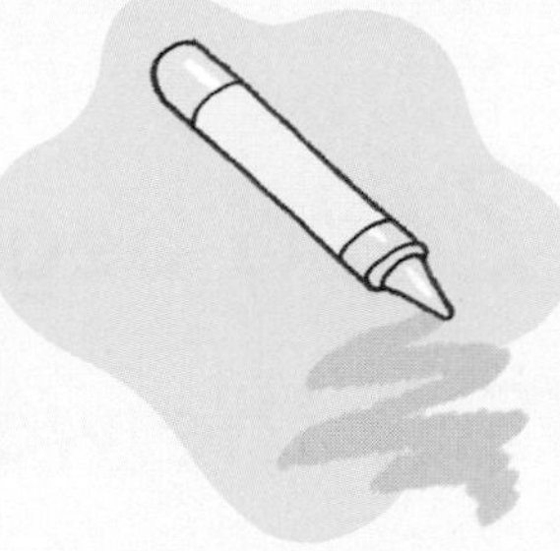

Xylophone begins with the X sound.
Yellow begins with the Y sound.

Say the word for each thing in the picture.

Circle the things that begin with the X sound or the Y sound.

Z as in Zero

Zero begins with the Z sound.

Say the word for each thing in the picture.

Circle the things that begin with the Z sound.

Vowels: A

Hat has the short A sound.
Baby has the long A sound.

Say the word for each picture.

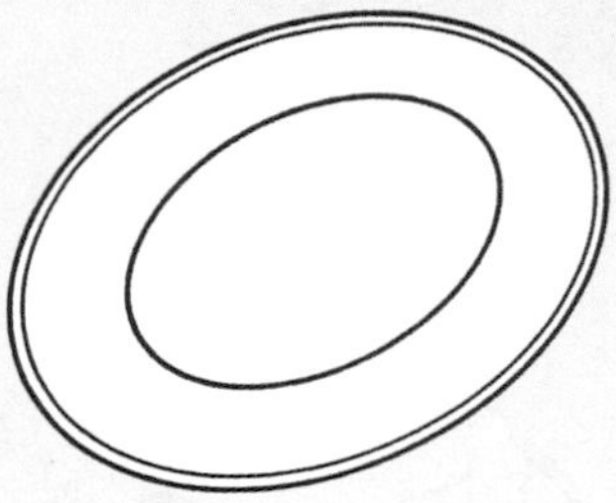

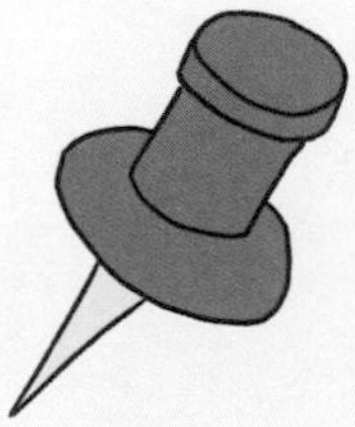

Use red to circle the pictures that have the same short A sound as hat.

Use green to circle the pictures that have the same long A sound as baby.

Vowels: E

Sled has the short E sound.
Eagle has the long E sound.

Say the word for each picture.

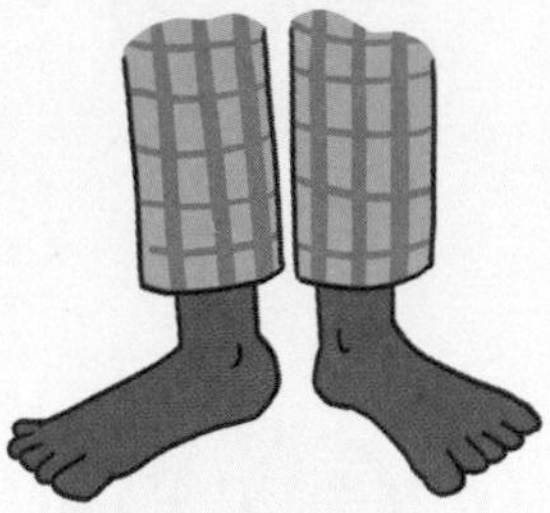

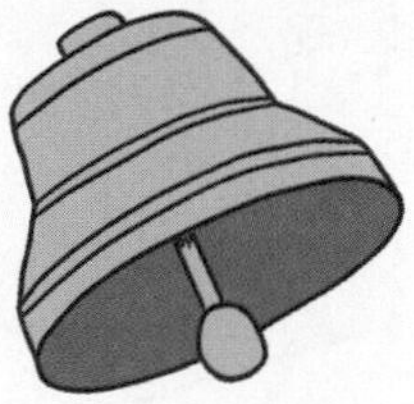

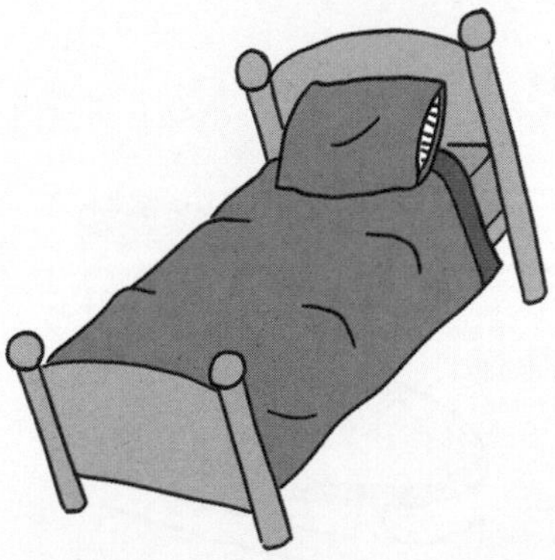

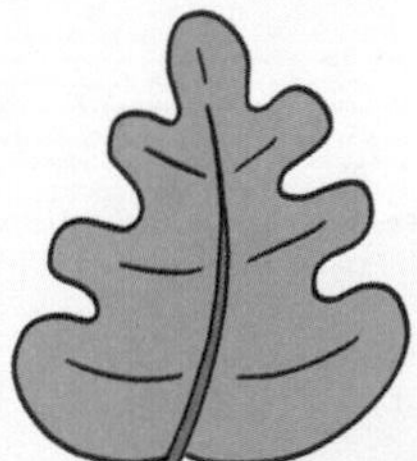

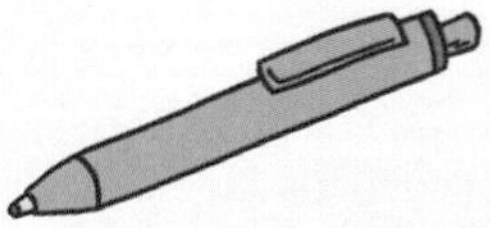

Use red to circle the pictures that have the same short E sound as sled.

Use green to circle the pictures that have the same long E sound as eagle.

Vowels: I

Pig has the short I sound.
Kite has the long I sound.

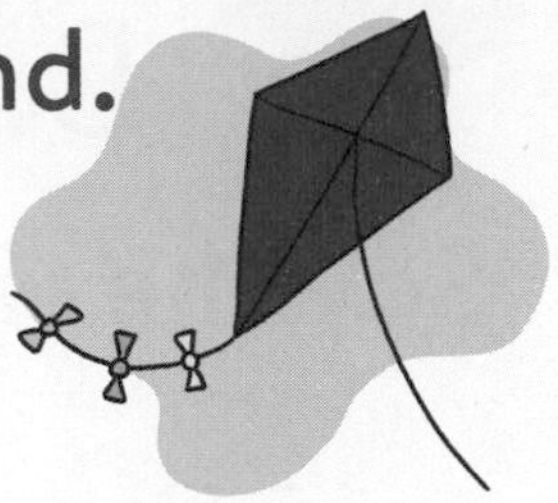

Say the word for each picture.

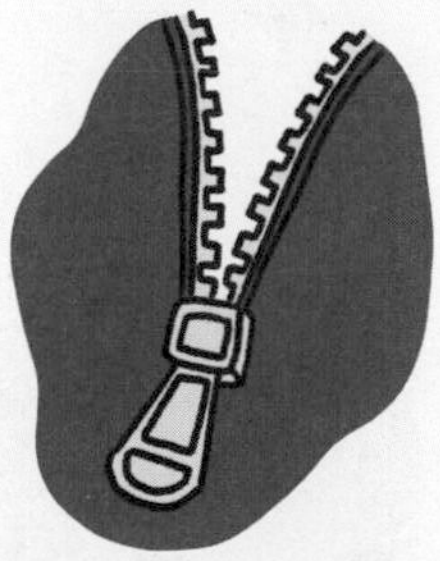

Use red to circle the pictures that have the same short I sound as pig.

Use green to circle the pictures that have the same long I sound as kite.

Vowels: O

Fox has the short O sound.

Boat has the long O sound.

Say the word for each picture.

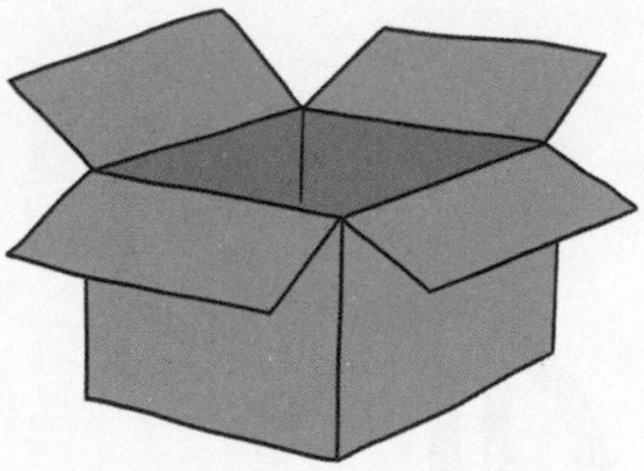

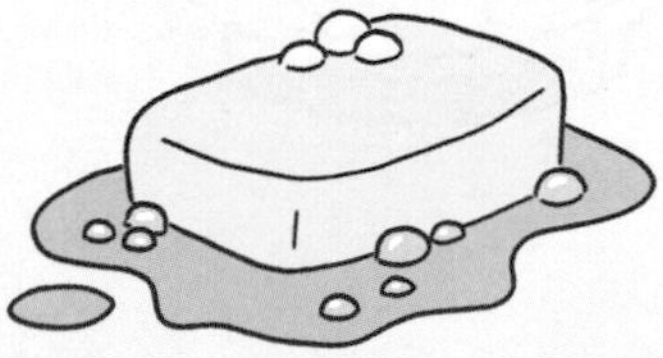

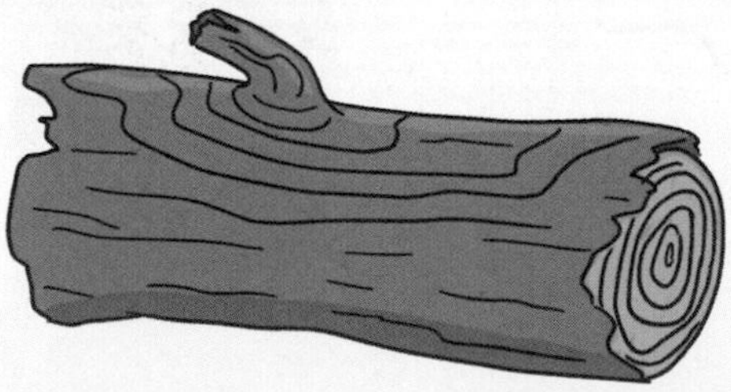

Use red to circle the pictures that have the same short O sound as fox.

Use green to circle the pictures that have the same long O sound as boat.

Vowels: U

Duck has the short U sound.

Glue has the long U sound.

Say the word for each picture.

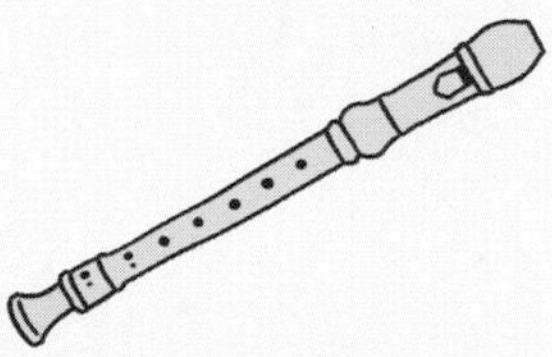

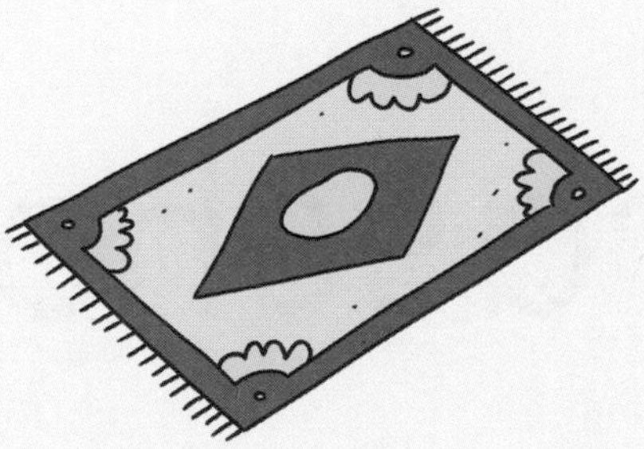

Use red to circle the pictures that have the same short U sound as duck.

Use green to circle the pictures that have the same long U sound as glue.

Bug Out!

Say the name of each creepy-crawly.

What is the first sound you hear?

Write the letter that makes that sound.

___adybug

___ee

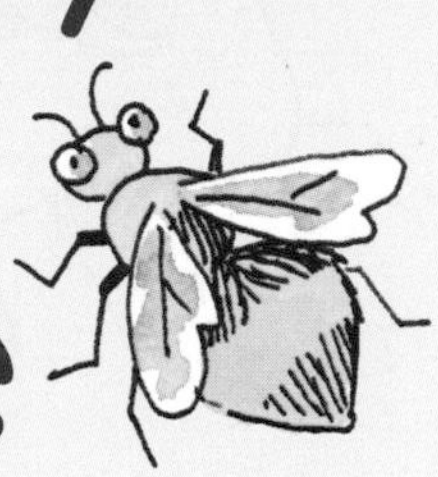

___rasshopper

___ly

___pider

My Stuff!

Say the word for each picture.

What is the first sound you hear?

Write the letter that makes that sound.

__otebook

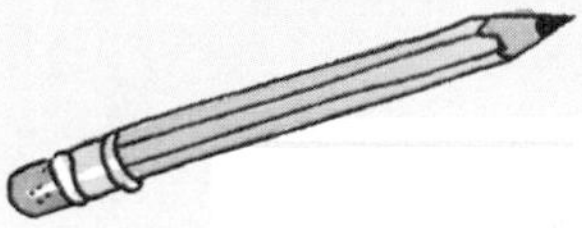

__encil

__ackpack

__uler

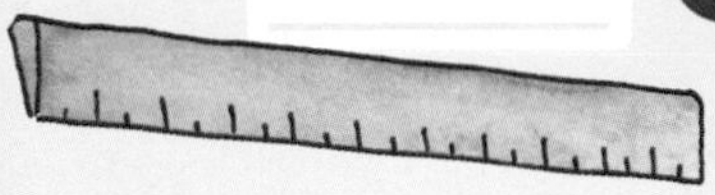

__rayons

PHONICS

My Toys

Say the name of each stuffed animal.

What is the first sound you hear?

Write the letter that makes that sound.

lephant

ebra

onkey

og

iger

Garden

Say the name of each object in the picture.

What is the first sound you hear in each word?

Write the letter that makes that sound.

Color!

Each picture rhymes with a color word.

Draw a line from each object to its rhyming color.

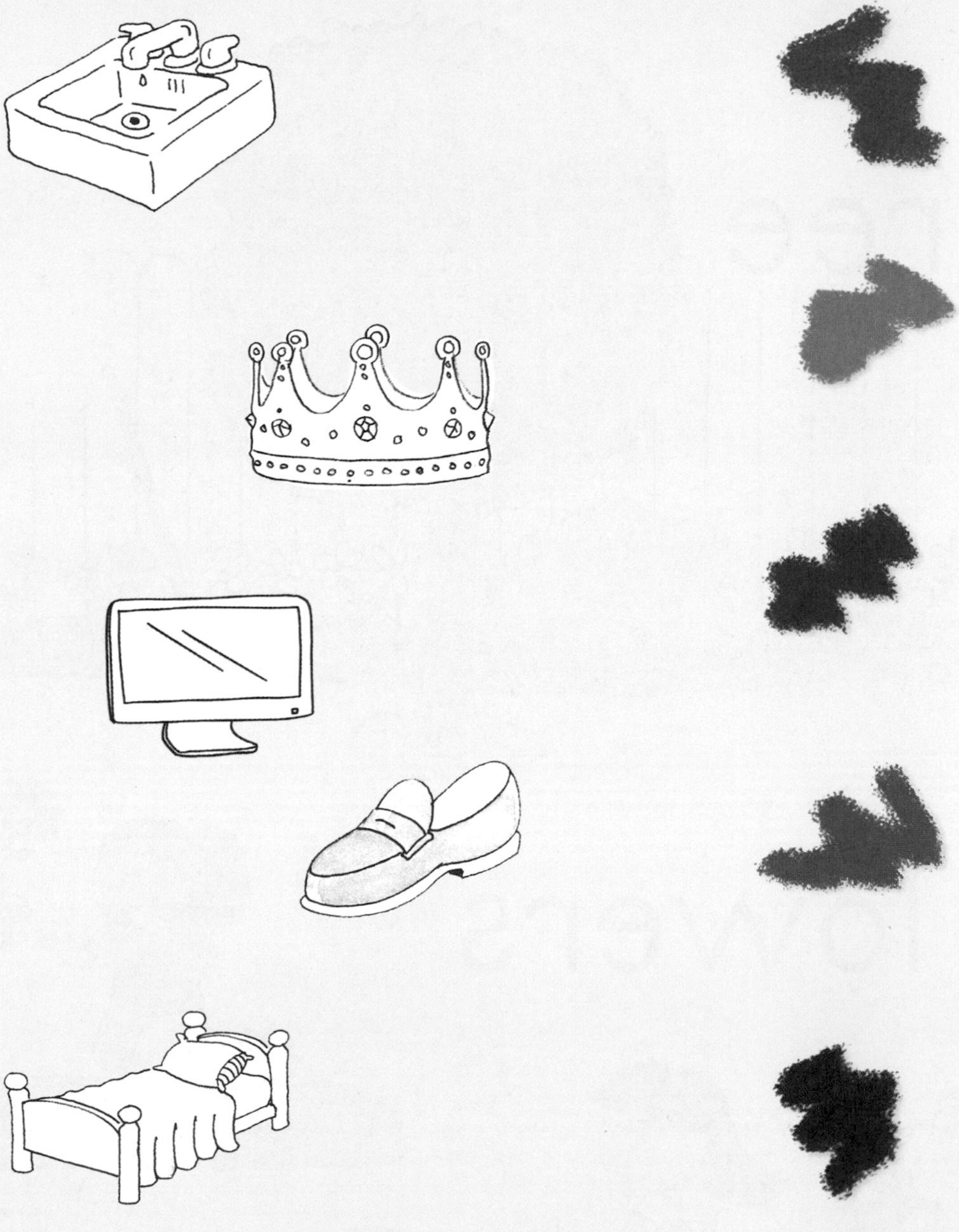

Now color each picture with its rhyming color!

Get Going!

The pictures on the left help us go.

The pictures on the right rhyme with them.

Draw a line to match the rhyming pictures.

Yard Sale!

Say the word for the items on each table.

Draw a line from an item on one table to a rhyming item on the other table.

Animals

Draw a line to match each animal to the picture that rhymes with them.

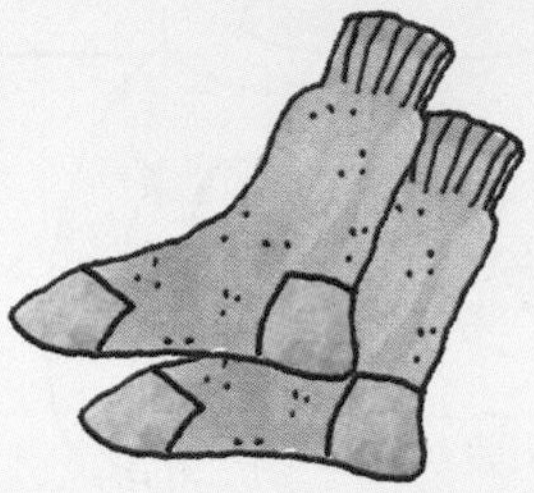

SPELLING AND VOCABULARY

You've learned the letter sounds. Now it's time to s-p-e-l-l! Let's put letters together to make words.
CAT
G
E
H
J

PARENTS Sight words are non-decodable words that occur frequently in English like *I*, *you*, *the*. In this section, your child will practice recognizing these words by sight until they "just know" how to spell them. Learning to spell helps children become stronger readers.

PLACE A STICKER HERE

For additional resources, visit www.BrainQuest.com/kindergarten

I

Say the word I.

Trace and then write the word I.

Write I to complete the sentences.

____ am a child.

____ like to learn.

____ like to play.

my

Say the word my.

Trace and then write the word my.

my my

Write my to complete the sentences.

This is ______ favorite color:

Color the box your favorite color.

This is ______ name:

Write your name here.

you

Say the word **you**.

Trace and then write the word **you**.

you you

Write **you** to complete the sentences.

Are ______ happy?

Are ______ sad?

Are ______ funny?

and

Say the word and.

Trace and then write the word and.

and and

The word and connects words.

Write and to connect these opposites.

day ______ night

empty ______ full

left ______ right

a

Say the word a.

Trace and then write the word a.

a a

These children are dressed in costumes!
Write a to tell about them.

I am ___ pirate!

I am ___ fairy!

I am ___ dragon!

I am ___ ghost!

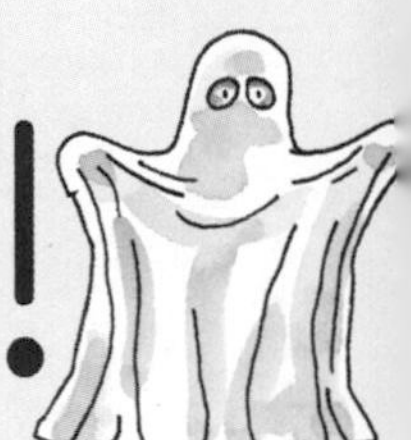

the

Say the word **the**.

Trace and then write the word **the**.

the the

Write **the** to label the animals.

cat 

dog 

fish 

hamster 

is

Say the word is.

Trace and then write the word is.

is is

Write is to tell about the weather.

It ______ sunny today.

It ______ rainy today.

are

Say the word are.

Trace and then write the word are.

are are

What are these monsters doing?

Write are to tell about them.

The monsters ____ dancing.

The monsters ____ singing.

he

Say the word he.

Trace and then write the word he.

he he

The word he tells about a boy.

Meet Mike! Write he to tell about Mike.

Does ______ like to paint?

Yes, ______ likes to paint.

she

Say the word she.

Trace and then write the word she.

she she

The word she tells about a girl.

Meet Maya! Write she to tell about Maya.

Does ______ like to play soccer?

Yes, ______ likes to play soccer.

SPELLING AND VOCABULARY

see

Say the word **see**.

Trace and then write the word **see**.

see see

The astronauts are in space.

Write **see** to tell about what they see.

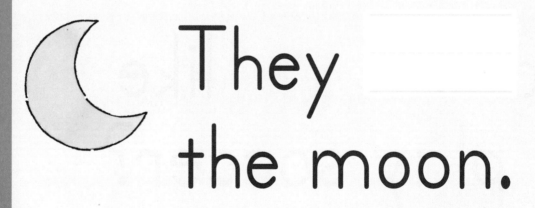

They ______ the moon.

They ______ the Earth!

go

Say the word go.

Trace and then write the word go.

go go

Where is this family going?

Write go to tell about their trip.

They ______ to the beach.

They ______ on the rides.

Sight Words

Practice reading sight words by making your own flash cards at home!

I	my	you
and	a	the
is	are	he
she	see	go

123s

APRIL
1 2 3 4 5 6 7
8 9 10 11 12 13 14
15 16 17 18 19 20 21
22 23 24 25 26 27 28
29 30 31
How old are you now? How old will you be next year . . . and the year after that? Every day, we count and use math. 3-2-1, let's go!

PARENTS Remind your child that numbers are everywhere! Extend their learning by counting things you find or do during the day, like "How many blocks are in this tower?" or "How many carrots are left on the plate?"

PLACE A STICKER HERE

1 one

Trace the number 1.

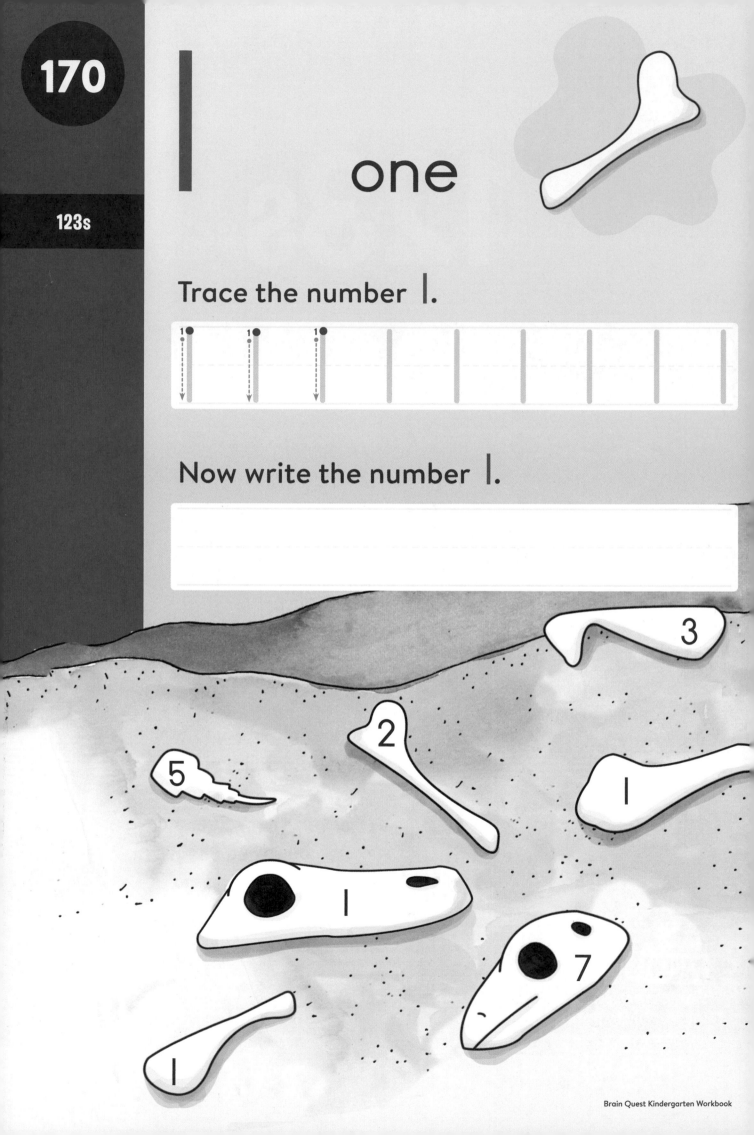

Now write the number 1.

Help the scientist find dinosaur bones.

Color the bones that have the number 1.

2 two

Trace the number 2.

Help the kids get to the zoo!

Draw a line down the street with the number 2.

Now write the number 2.

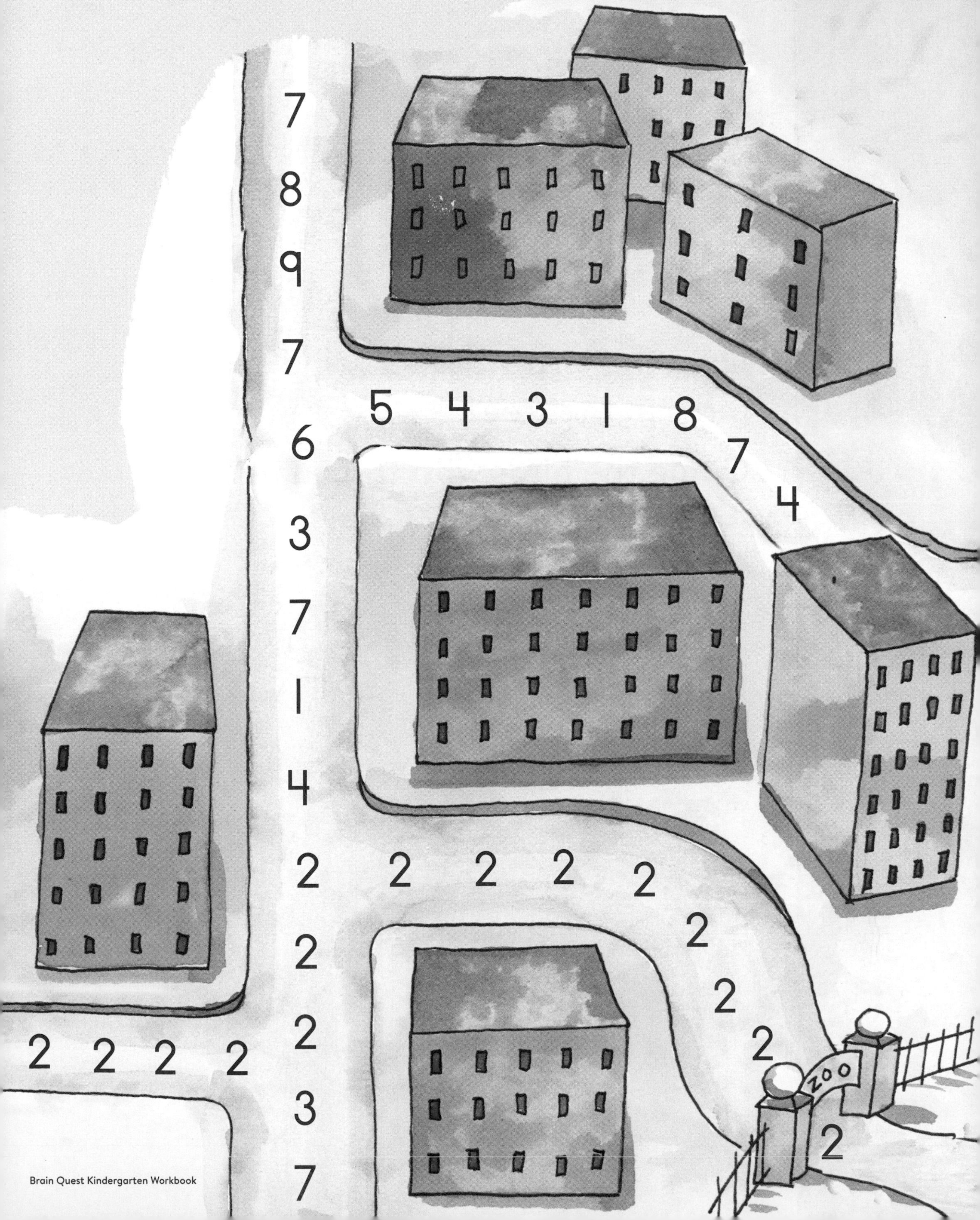

3 three

Trace the number 3.

Help the bird-watchers find the birds in the tree.

Circle the birds with the number 3.

Now write the number 3.

4 four

Trace the number 4.

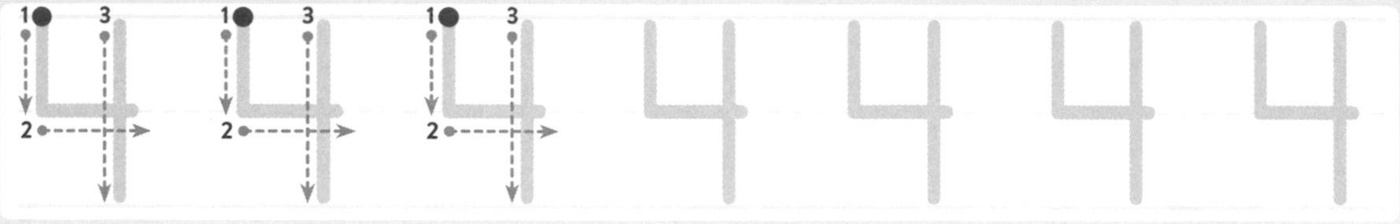

Now write the number 4.

Which monsters live at 4 Monster Lane?

Draw a line from each monster with the number 4 to the house.

5 five

Trace the number 5.

Help Mario celebrate his birthday!
Circle each number 5 on the cake.

Now write the number 5.

6

six

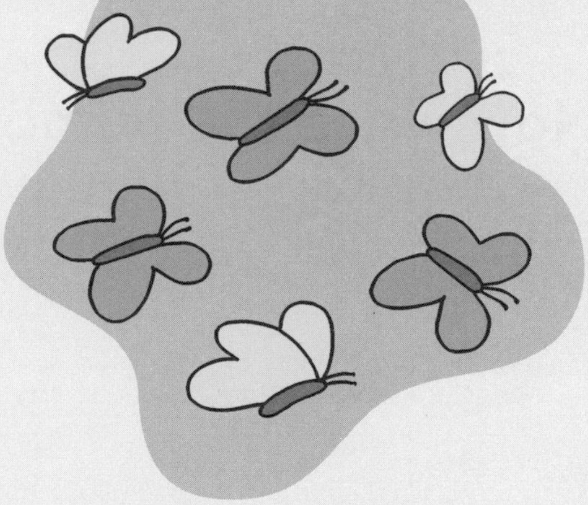

Trace the number 6.

6 6 6 6 6 6 6

Now write the number 6.

This family is watching butterflies.

Circle each butterfly with the number 6 on it.

7 seven

Trace the number 7.

Help the race car driver win this race!

Draw a line down the path with the number 7.

Now write the number 7.

8

eight

Trace the number 8.

8 8 8 8 8 8 8

Now write the number 8.

Grandpa's favorite number is 8.

Circle each picture with the number 8 to show to Grandpa.

9 nine

Trace the number 9.

Now write the number 9.

Help the monkey climb the tree.

Draw a line up the vine with the number 9.

9 9 9 9 9 9 9 9 9 9 9 9 9 9 9 9 9 9 9 9 9 9 9 9 9 9 9 9 9 9 9 9 9 9 9 9
3 8 7 2 4
1 8 2 4
2 1 2 6
3 5 8 1 2
7 3 8 1 4 5 2
2 5 1
2 6 7 5 3 1 8
2 6 1

10 ten

Trace the number 10.

10 10 10 10 10

What are these people looking at?
Color the spaces with the number 10.

Now write the number 10.

11 eleven

Trace the number 11.

Now write the number 11.

There are a lot of numbers at a volleyball game!

Circle each number 11 at this game.

12 twelve

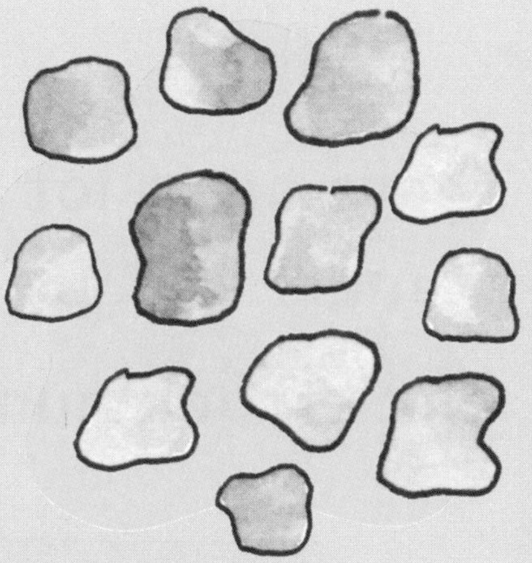

Trace the number 12.

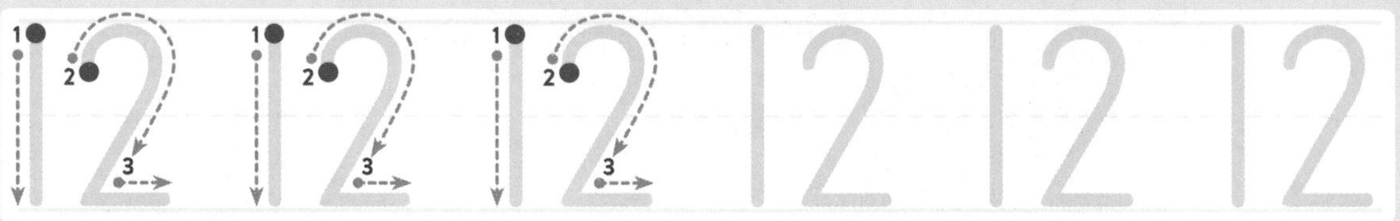

Help the traveler walk through the forest!

Draw a line down the path with the number 12.

Now write the number 12.

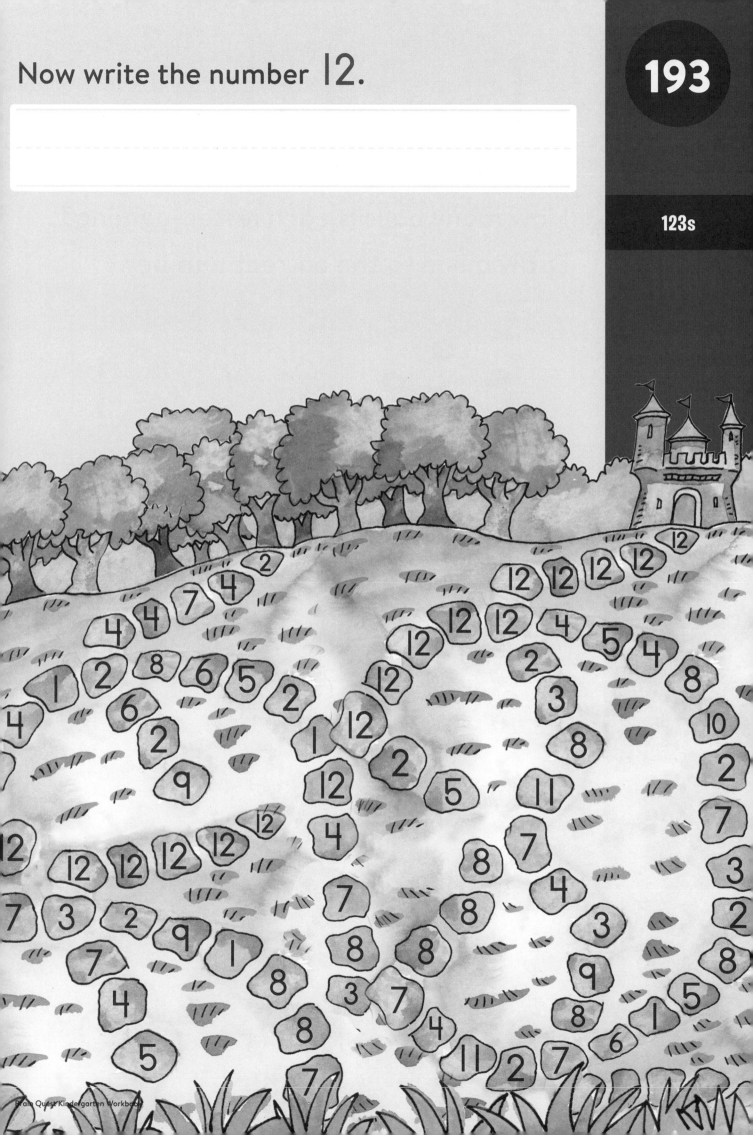

Juggle!

How many balls is each jester juggling?

Draw a line to the correct number.

1

2

3

4

5

Apples!

How many apples are in each group?

Draw a line to the correct number.

6

7

8

9

10

Lake Fun!

Count how many people and animals are in each group. Write the numbers on the lines.

Sports!

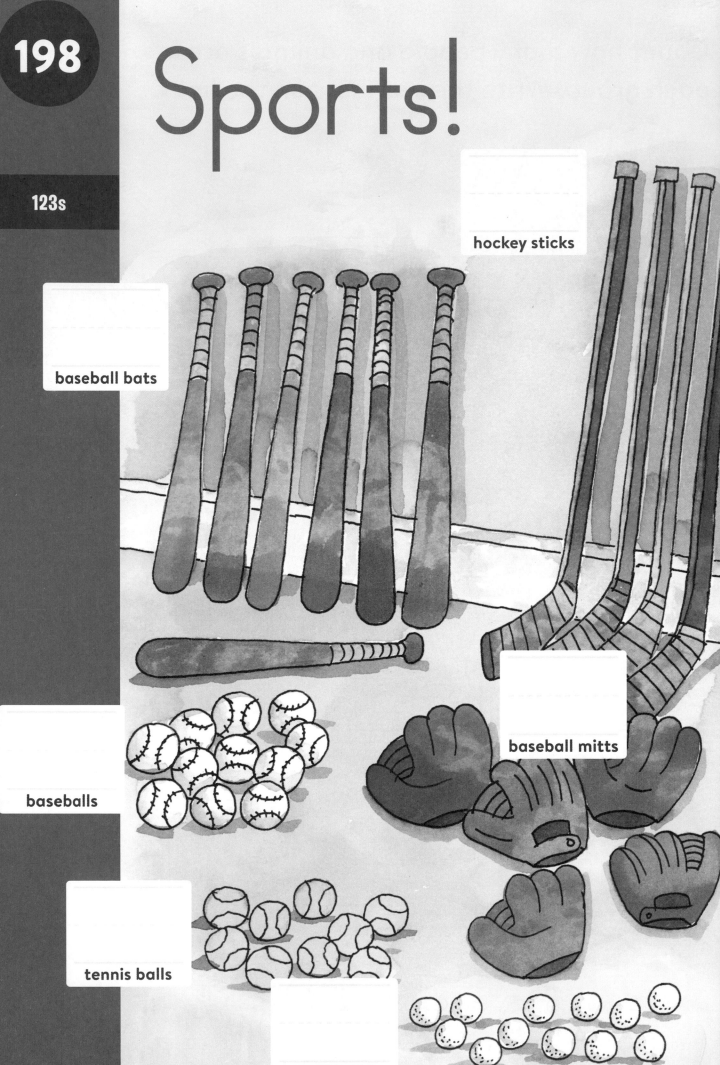

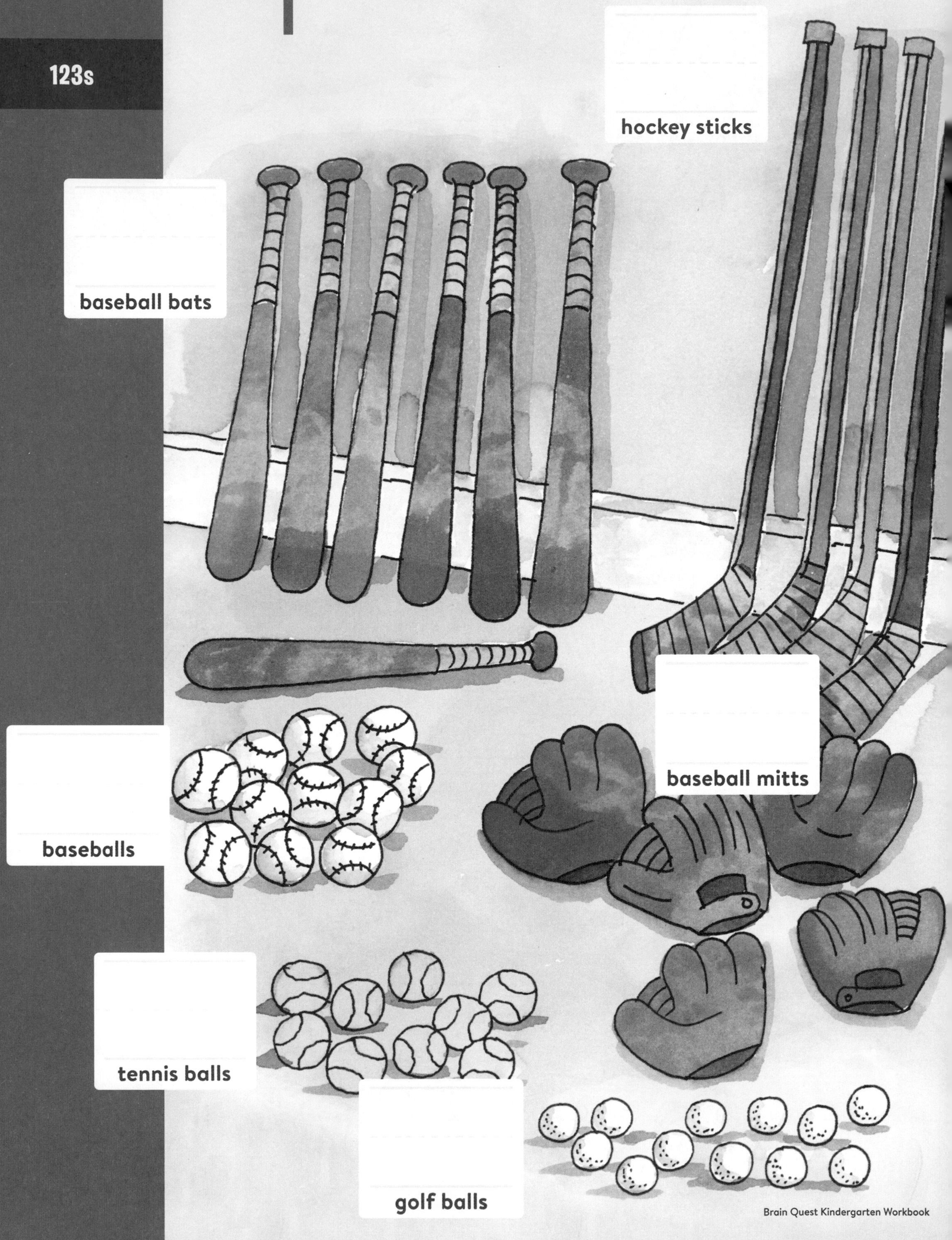
hockey sticks
baseball bats
baseball mitts
baseballs
tennis balls
golf balls

Count the sports gear in each group.

Write the numbers on the lines.

Toys!

dinosaurs
books
cubes
board games
dolls
tricycles
rocking horse

Count the toys in each group.

Write the numbers on the lines next to the toys.

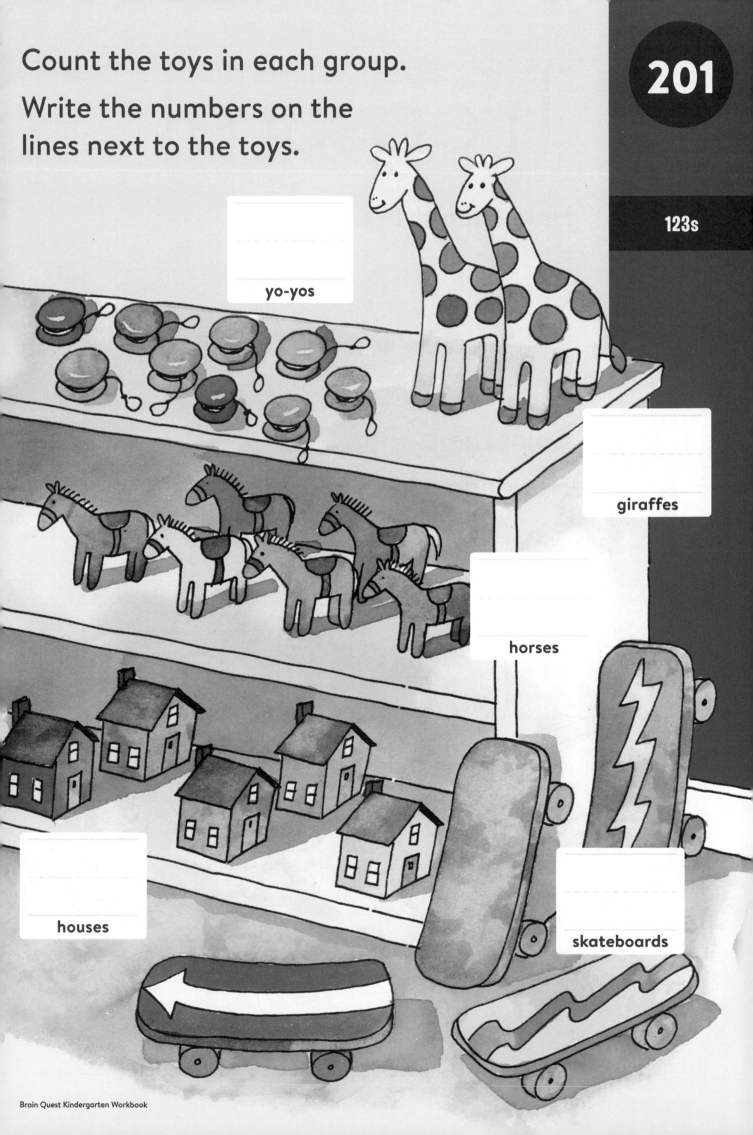

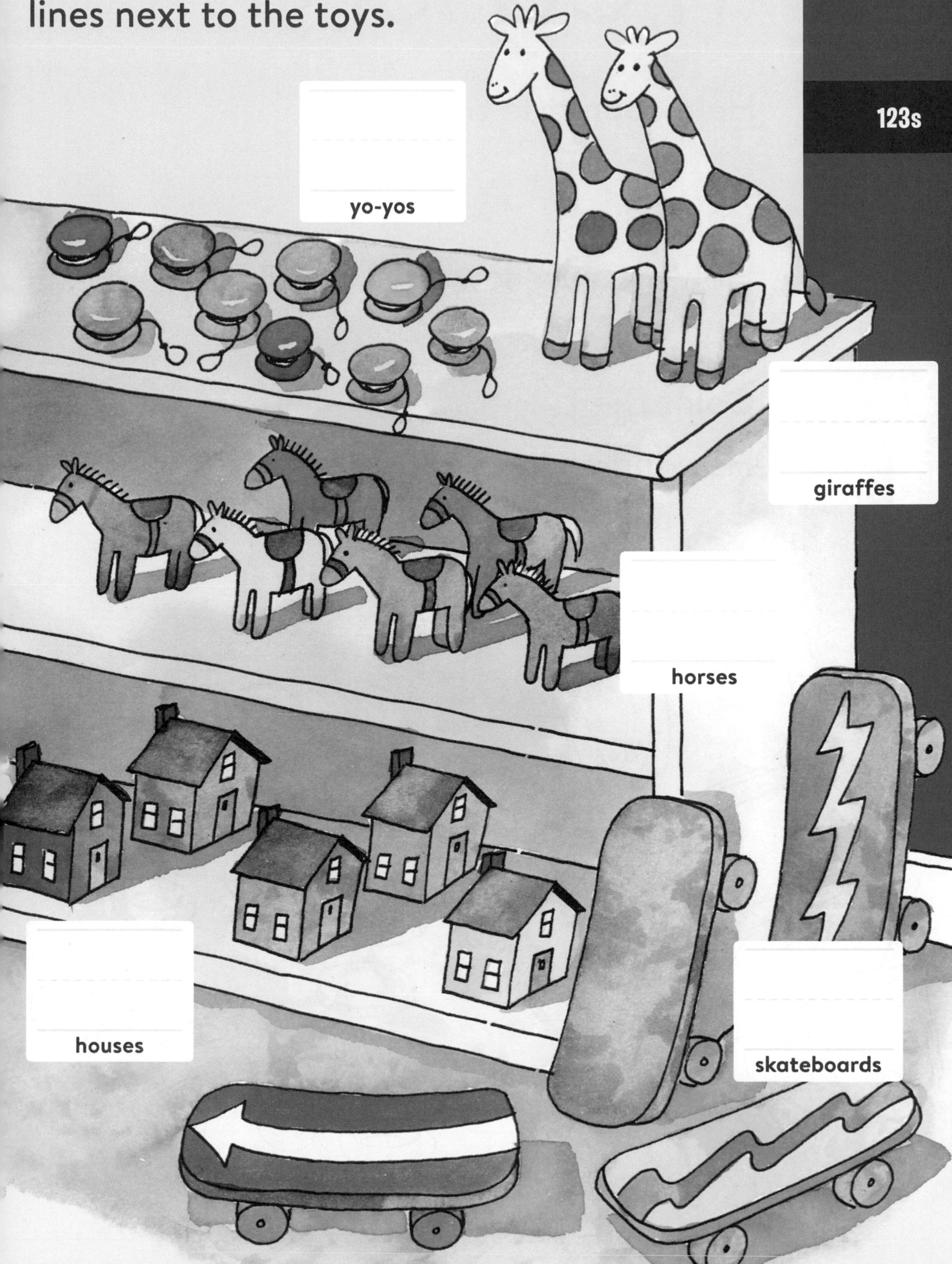

Treasure!

Help count the treasure!

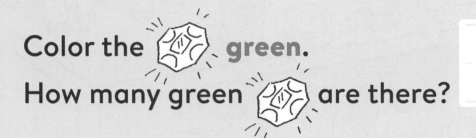

Color the  yellow.
How many yellow  are there?

Color the  green.
How many green  are there?

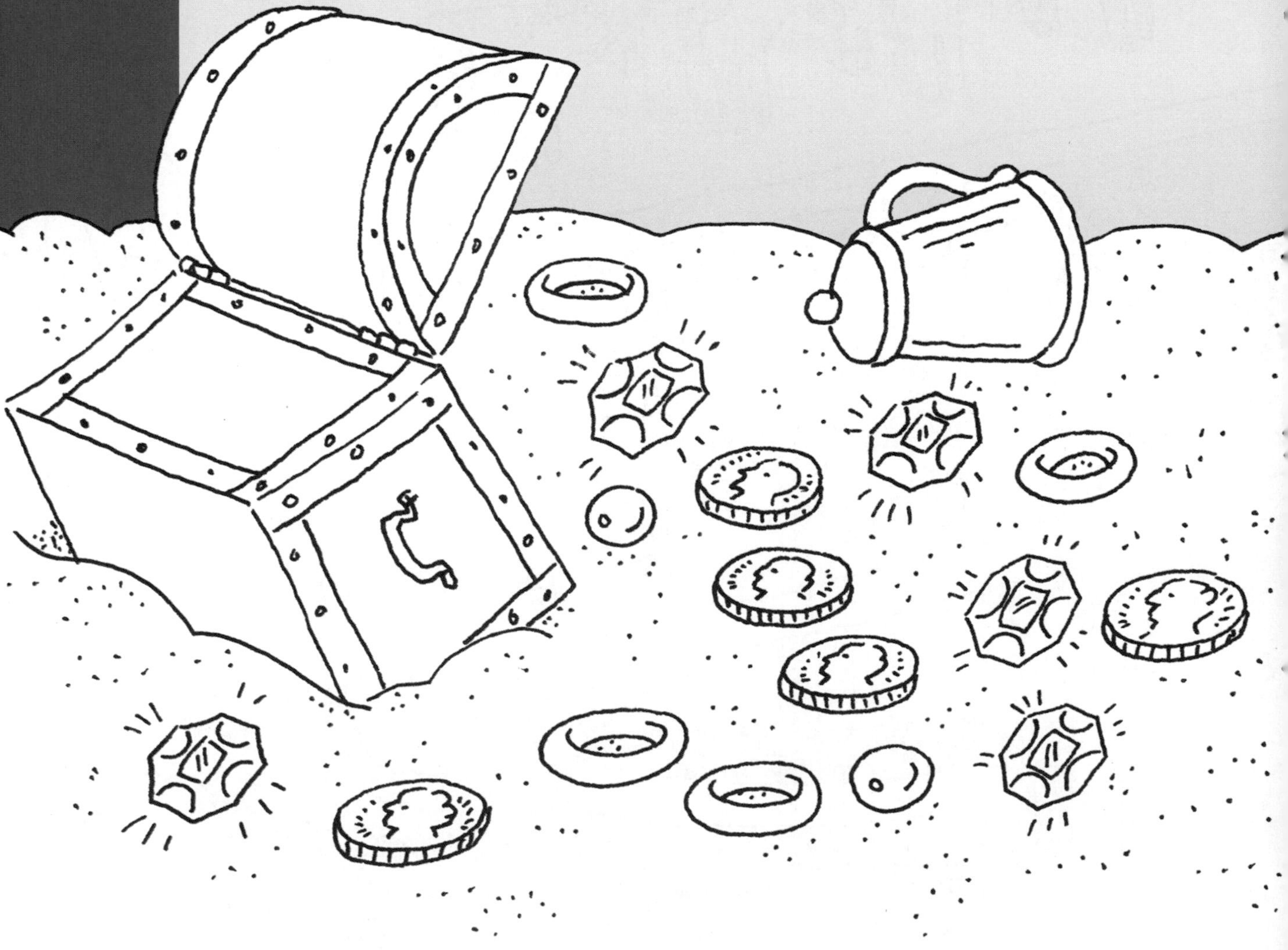

Color the pink.

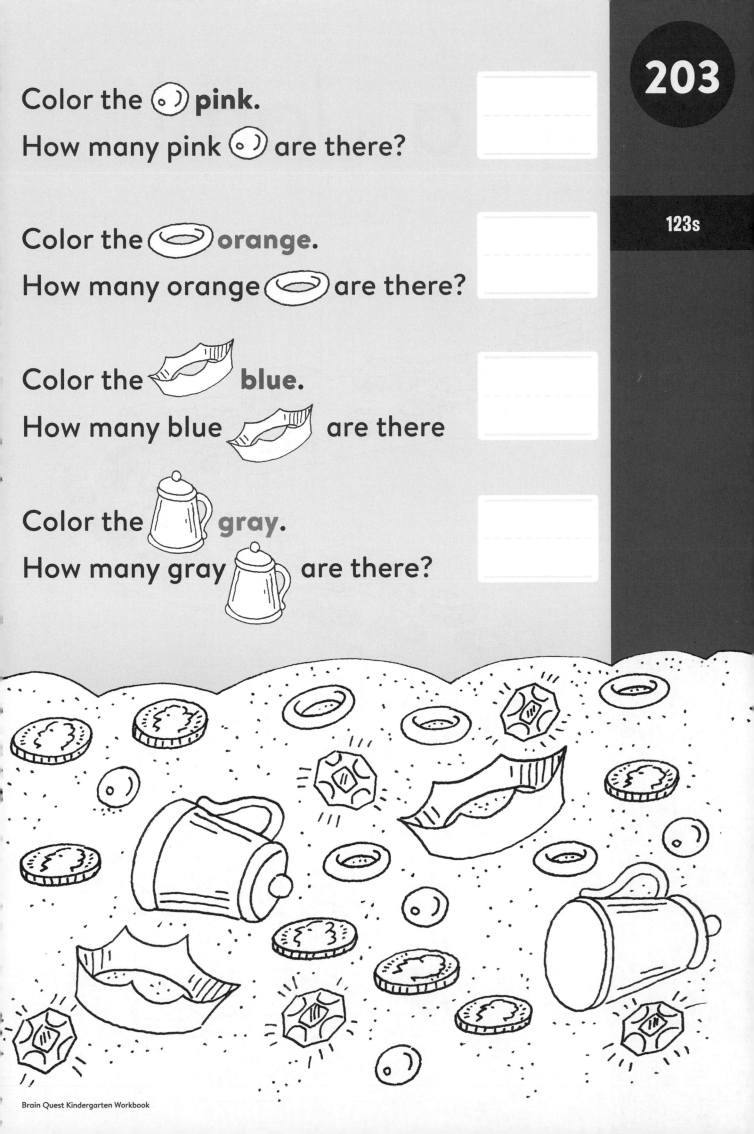

How many pink are there?

Color the orange.

How many orange are there?

Color the blue.

How many blue are there

Color the gray.

How many gray are there?

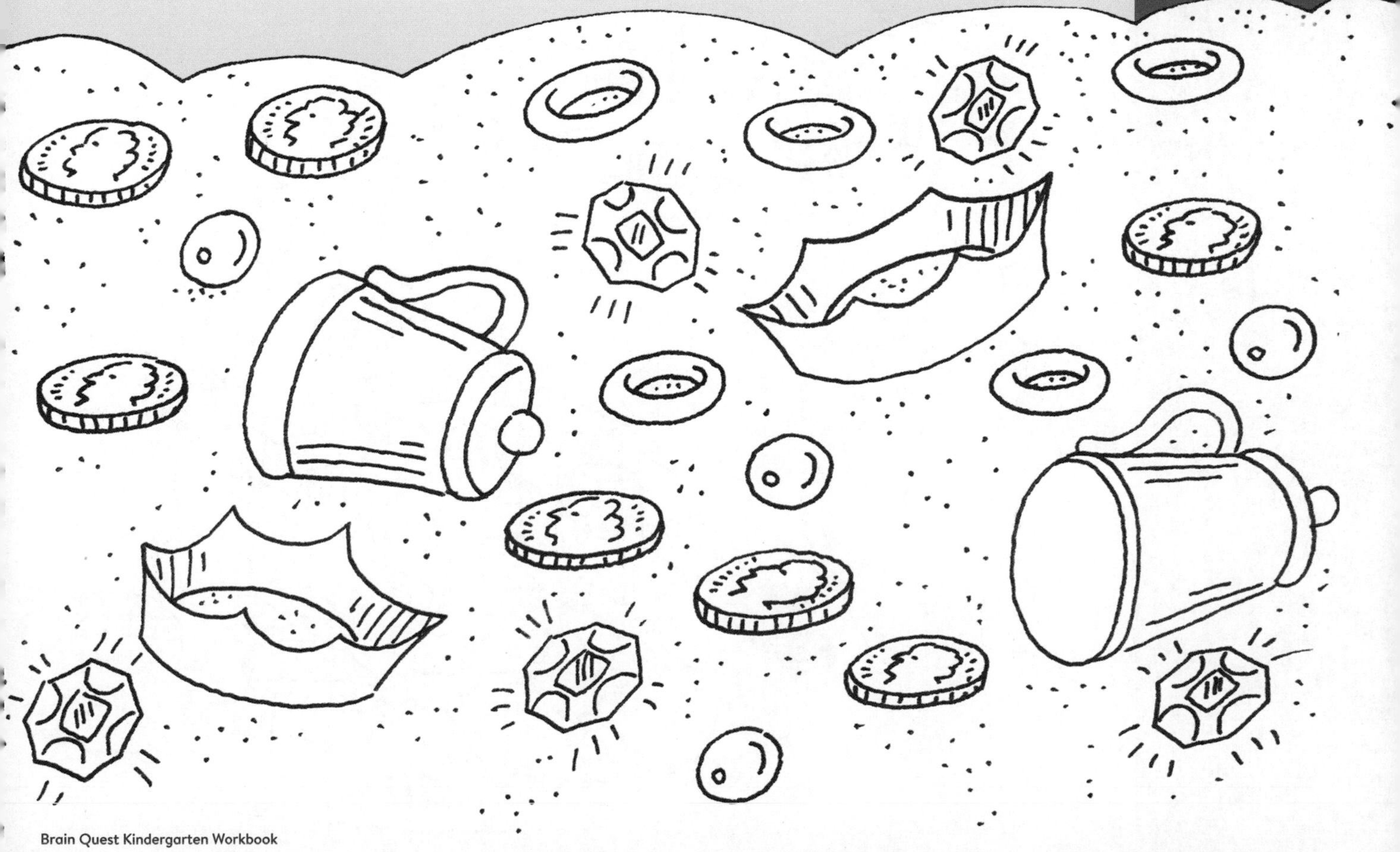

In a Jam!

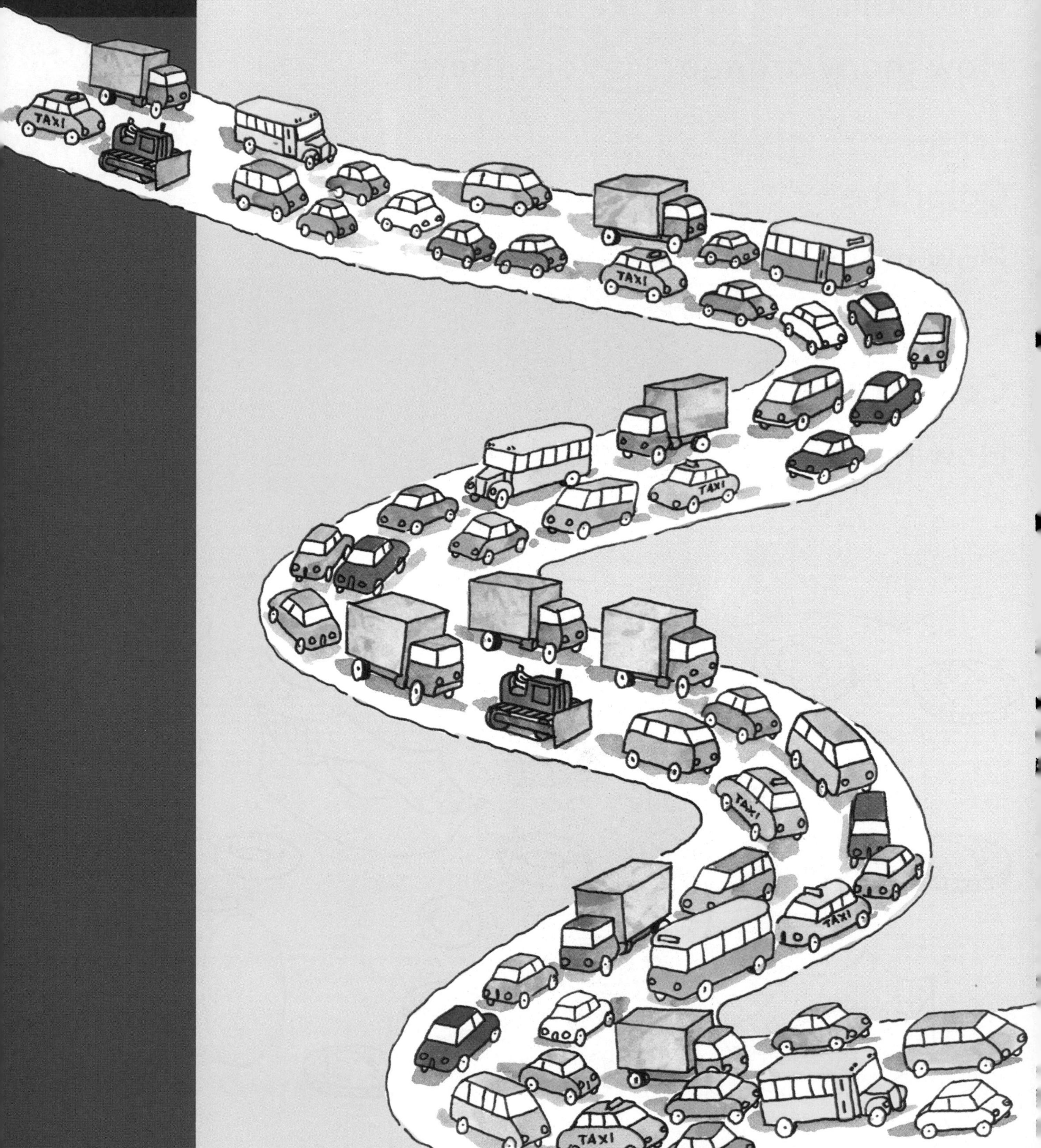

Count how many you see of each vehicle. Write the number on the line.

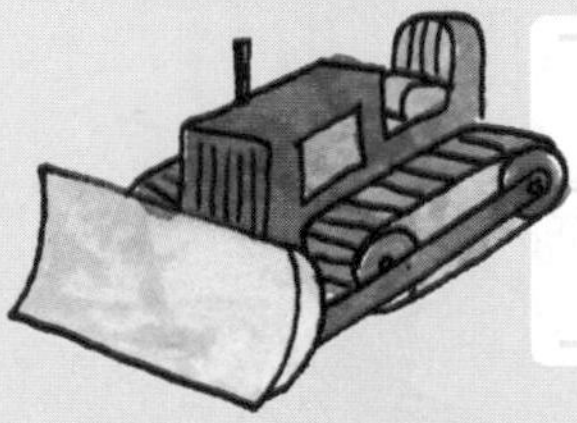

Snow Day

What do you see in the snow?

Count what you see!

Write the number on the line.

Scoops

Help serve the ice cream.

Draw the number of scoops on each cone.

COLORS AND SHAPES

What is your favorite color? What shape is your favorite toy? Knowing colors and shapes helps us describe the world around us. Let's learn more about colors and shapes.

PARENTS In this section, your child will learn colors and shapes following step-by-step directions. Help your child find and name shapes in the kitchen, in books you read, while playing with toys, or when you're outdoors together.

PLACE A STICKER HERE

For additional resources, visit www.BrainQuest.com/kindergarten

Buy It!

Let's look in the store.

Color the foods at the store.

Color the grapes **purple.**

Color the apples **red.**

Color the carrots **orange.**

Color the peppers **green.**

Color the blueberries **blue.**

Color the bananas **yellow.**

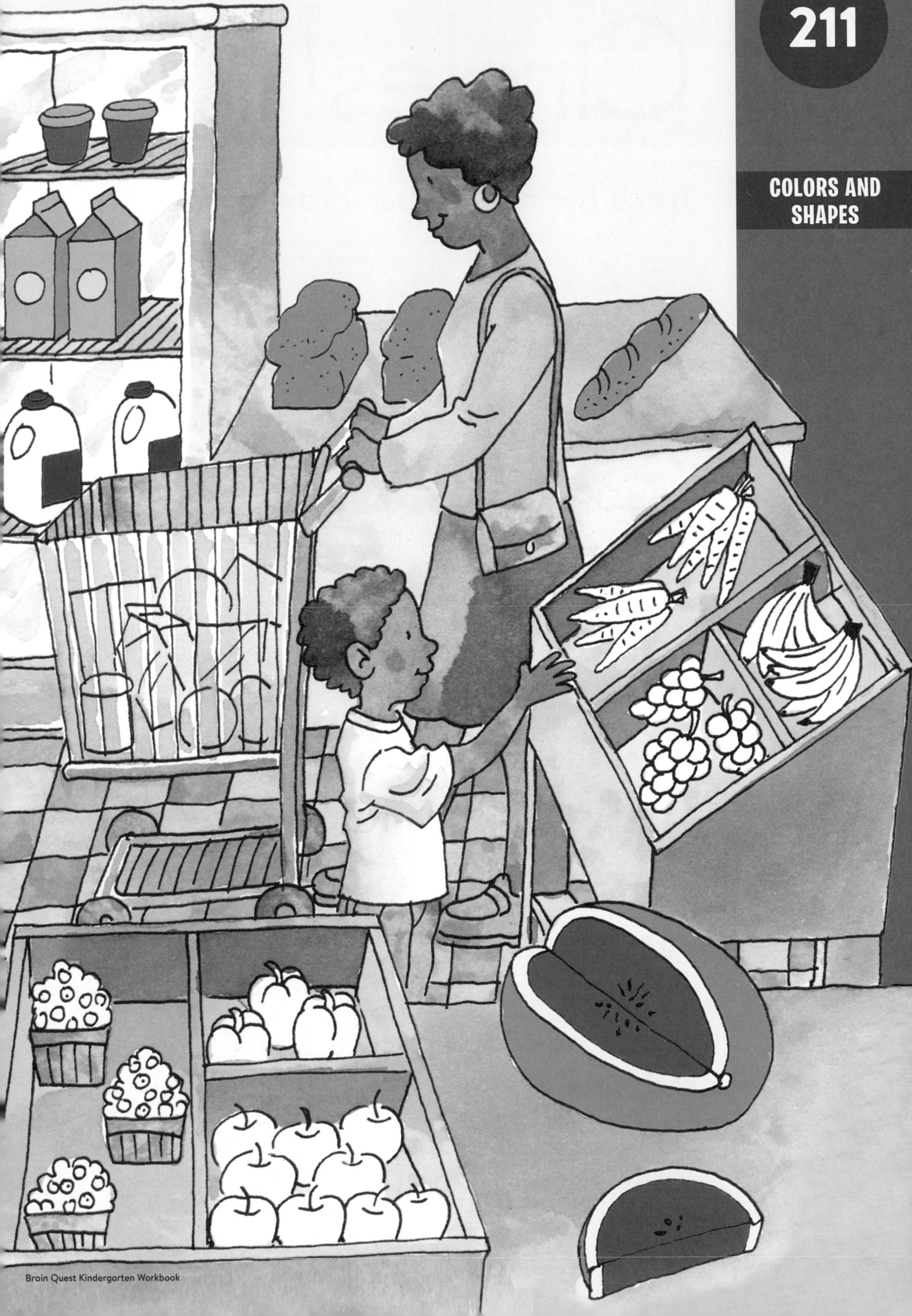

Circles!

Trace the circle. Then draw your own.

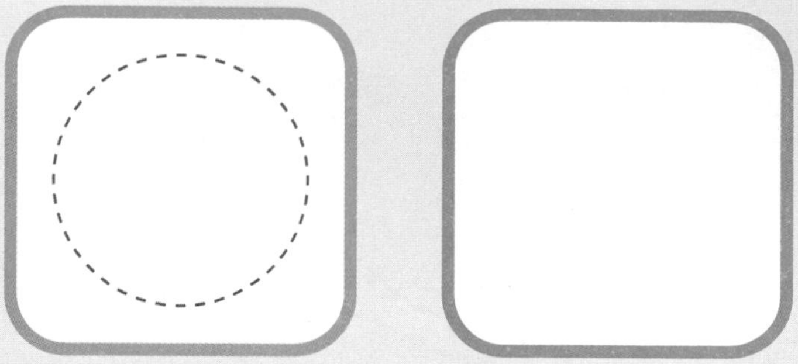

Find the circles at the playground.

Color the basketball **orange.**

Color the tennis ball **yellow.**

Color the baseball **purple.**

Color the soccer ball **red.**

Color the beach ball **blue** and **green.**

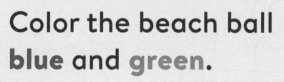

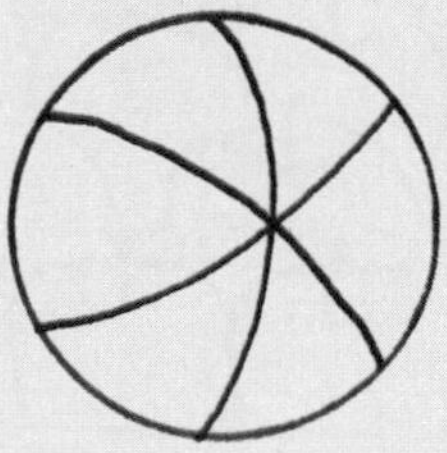

Squares!

Trace the square. Then draw your own.

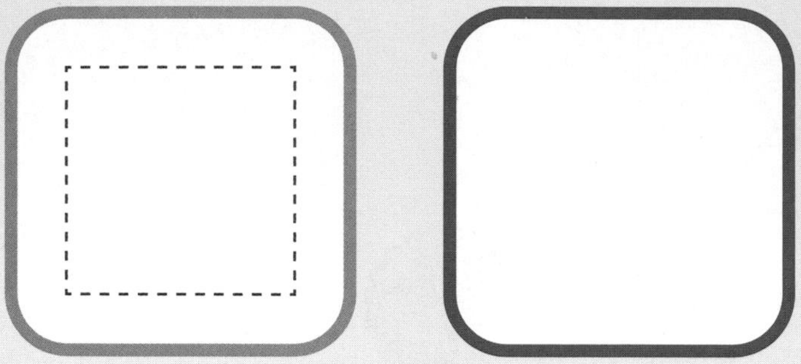

Find all the squares in the room.

Color the picture frames **brown.**

Color the jack-in-the-box **purple.**

Color the clock face **tan.**

Color the present **green** and **yellow**.

12
9
3
6

Triangles!

Trace the triangle. Then draw your own.

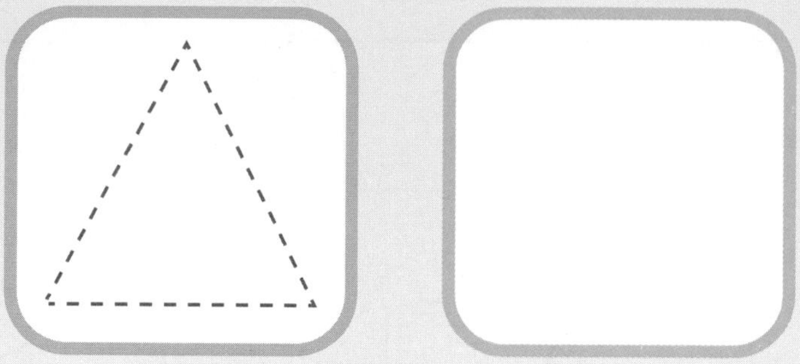

Circle the **red** triangle in each house.

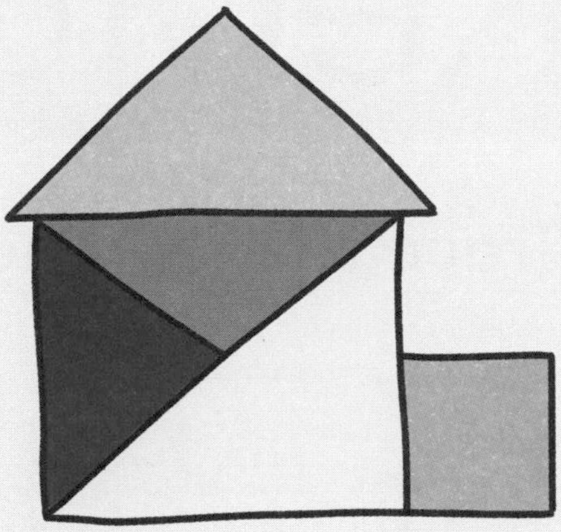

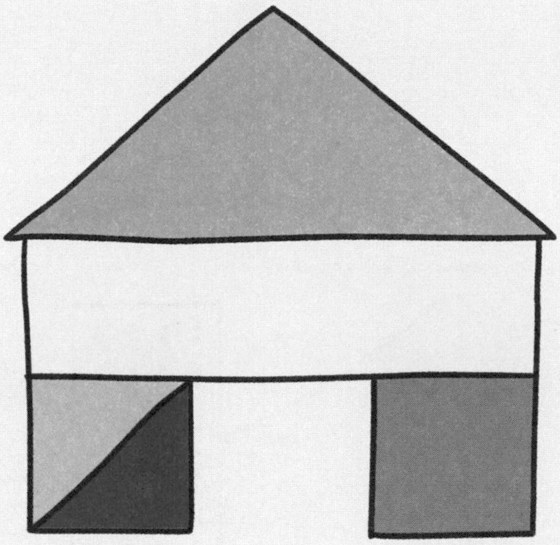

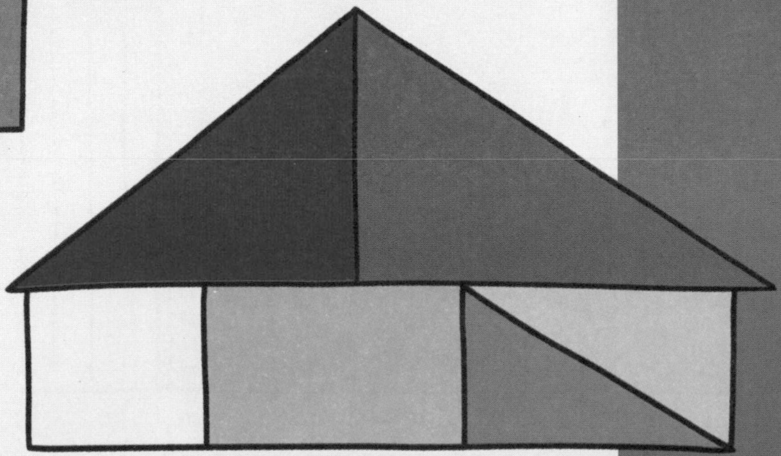

Rectangles!

Trace the rectangle. Then draw your own.

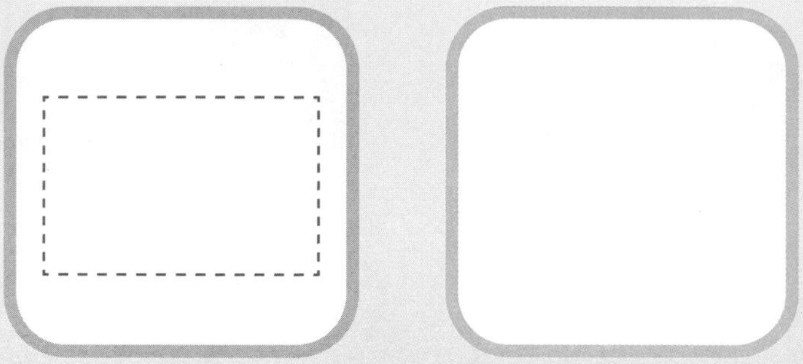

Count all the rectangles in this picture.

How many do you see?

Diamonds and Stars!

Trace the diamond. Trace the star.

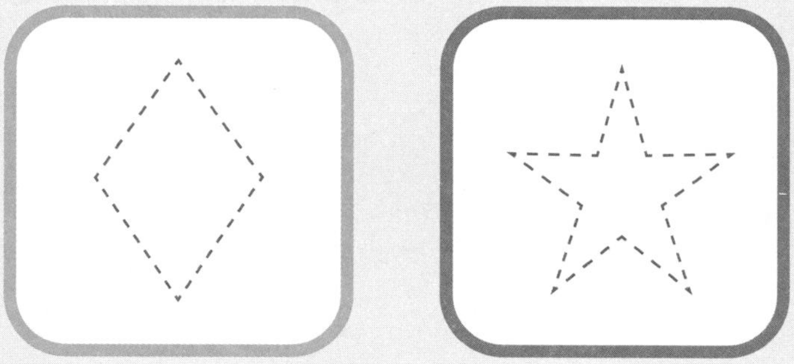

Circle all the diamonds and stars in the picture.

Shapes!

There are so many shapes!

Draw a line to match the shapes.

Robots!

Bring this robot to life!

Color the circles **blue.** 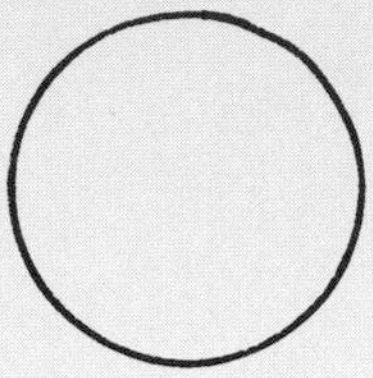

Color the stars **purple.** 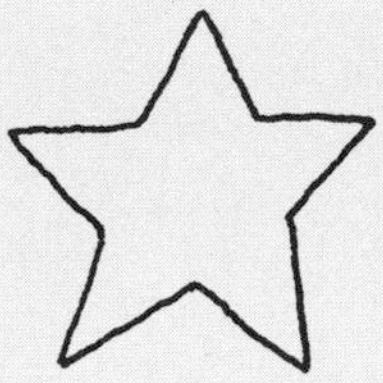

Color the triangles **yellow.** 

Color the rectangles **red.** 

Color the diamonds **green.** 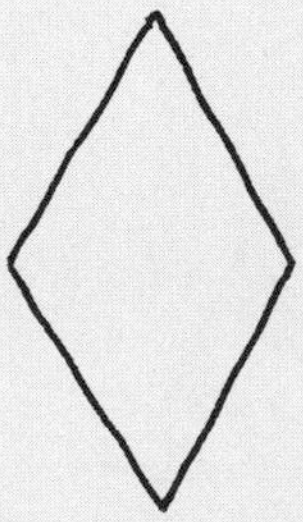

Color the squares **gray.** 

3D Shapes!

Trace the word for each shape.

cube

sphere

pyramid

PATTERNS

When colors, shapes, letters, sounds, or numbers repeat in the same order, it is called a pattern. Our world is full of patterns, like stripes on a flag, petals on a flower, and spots on a ladybug. Let's learn more about patterns.

PARENTS In kindergarten, children learn AB and ABC patterns. Patterns are important in math, language, music, technology, and more. Talk about patterns you see when with your child, whether looking at colors in a block tower or types of fruit on a plate.

PLACE A STICKER HERE

For additional resources, visit www.BrainQuest.com/kindergarten

Cityscape

Look at each row of buildings.

Do you see a pattern in the shapes?

Use the pattern to draw the next building.

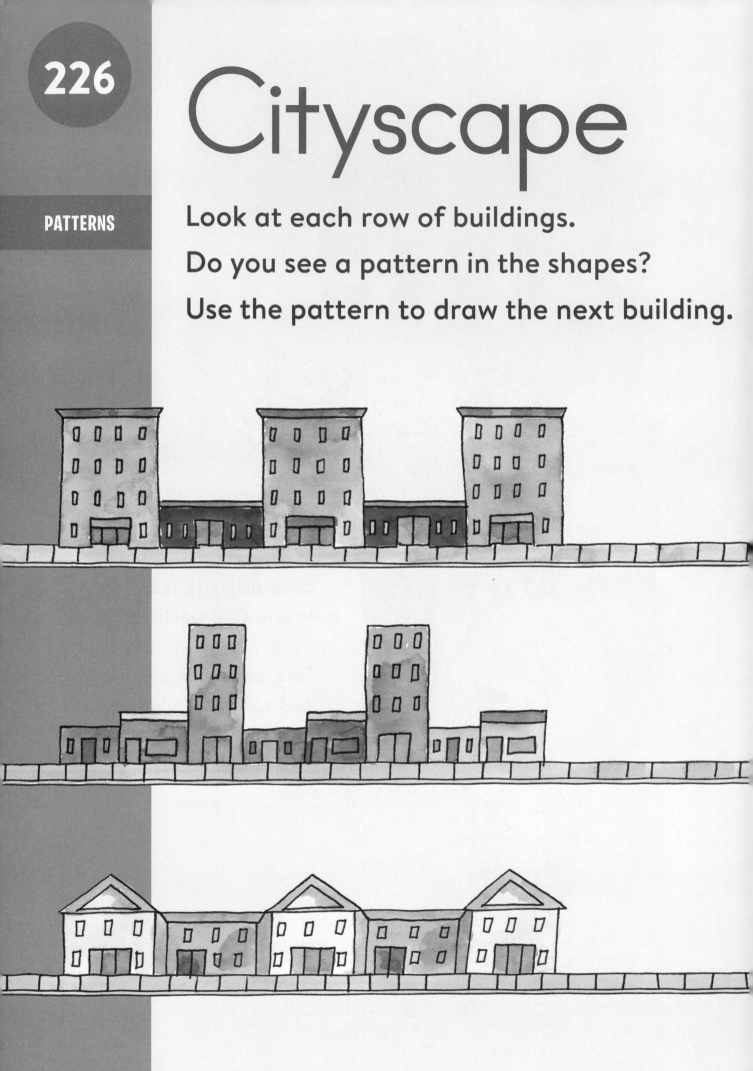

Night Sky

Look at the things in each row.

Do you see a pattern?

Use the pattern to draw the next object.

 ____

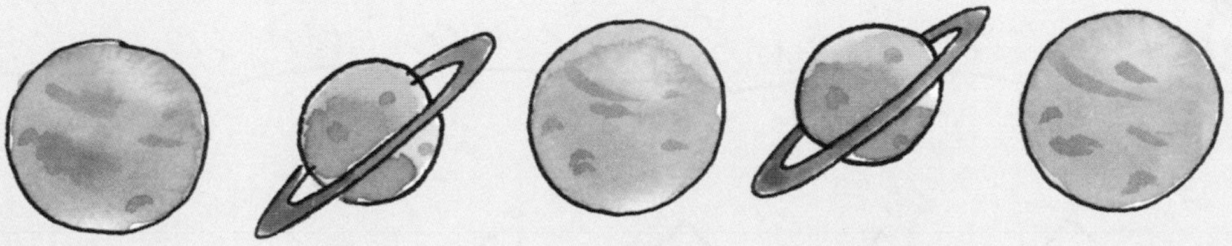 ____

 ____

Race Time!

Look at each row of shapes.

Do you see a pattern?

Use the pattern to finish each row.

Next One?

Look at each row of plants.

Do you see a pattern in the colors?

Use the pattern to color the white plants.

It's Teddy!

Look at the letters and numbers on the bear's shirt. Do you see a pattern?

Use the pattern to write the number or letter that comes next.

MATCHING AND SORTING

Matching means finding things that are alike. Sorting means putting things that are alike together. Let's find out what we can sort and match!

PARENTS Matching and sorting helps learners pay attention to details and organize visual information. They identify attributes of objects—shapes, colors, sizes, and more. You can reinforce this by matching socks or sorting silverware. Ask: How are these objects alike? What is different?

PLACE A STICKER HERE

The Desert

Help the animals find each other.

Draw a line to match the desert animals that are the same.

Farm Life!

Help these baby animals!

Draw a line to match each baby to its mother.

Leaves!

MATCHING AND SORTING

Some of these trees have the same kind of leaves.

Draw a line to match the trees with the same kind of leaves.

Pizza Party

Help the kids get their dinner!

Draw a line to match each child with the pizza they want.

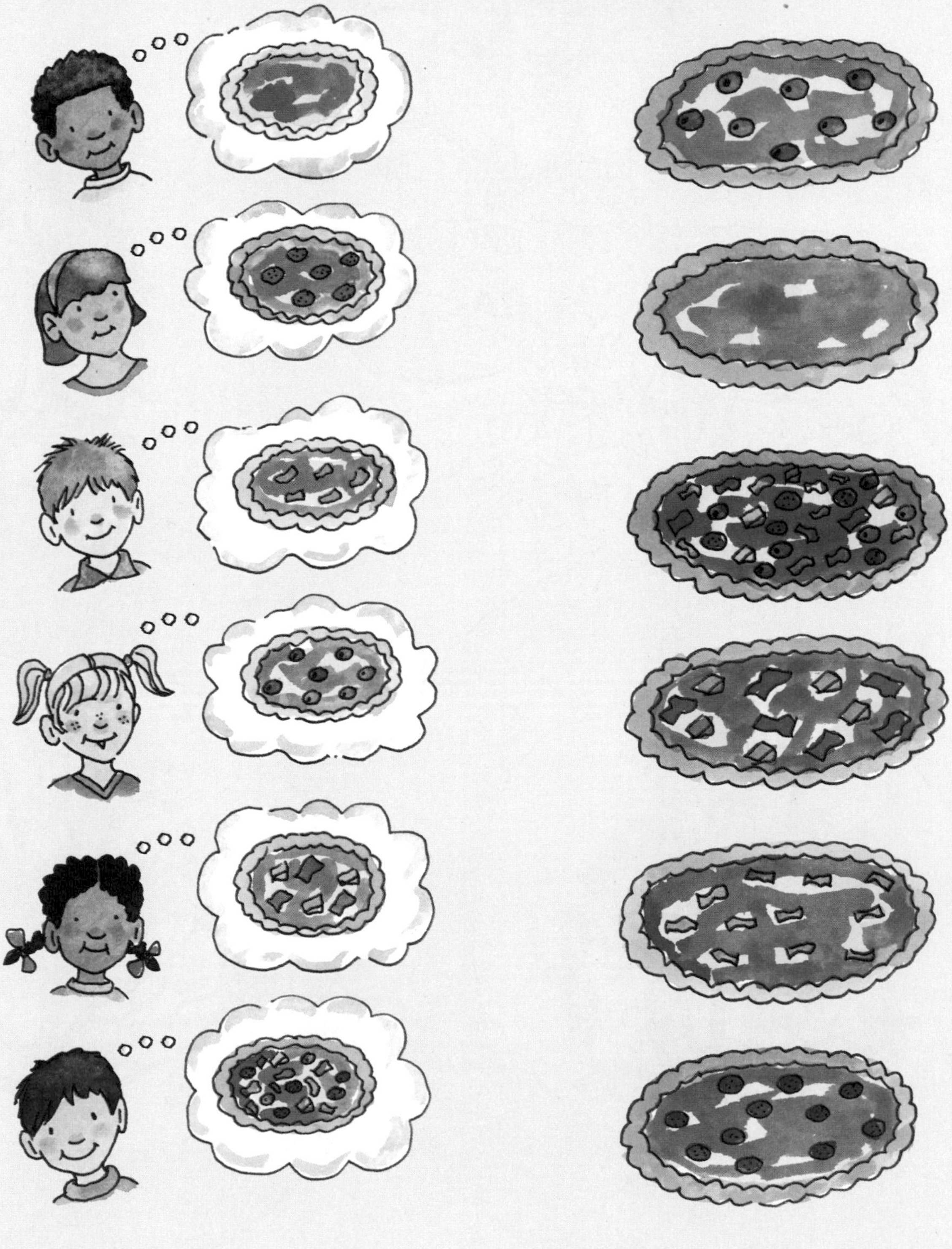

Going Home

Draw a line to match each animal to where you would find it.

Summer

It's hot out!

Circle the clothes you wear in the **summer.**

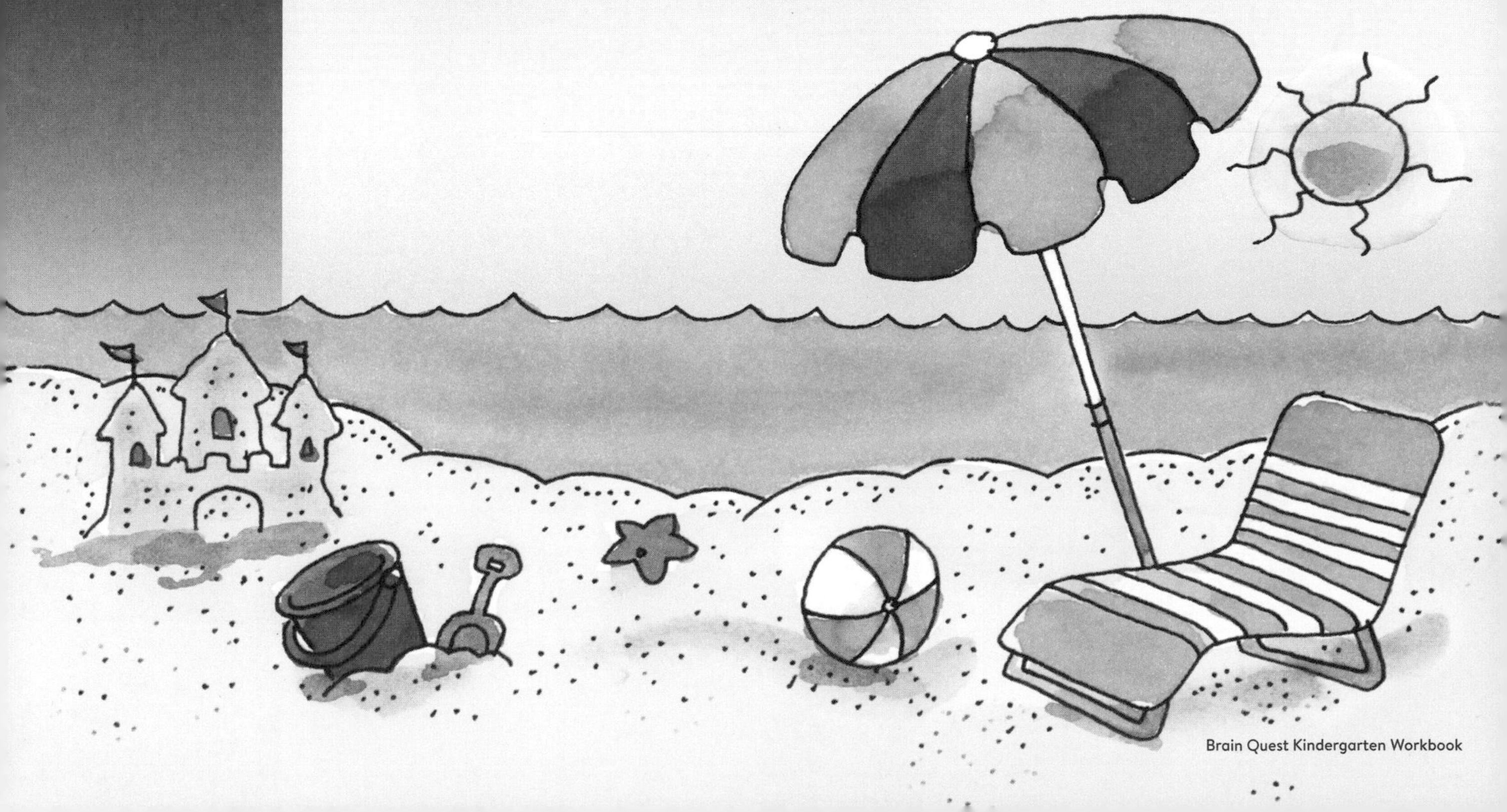

Winter

It's cold out!

Circle the clothes you wear in the **winter**.

The Arts!

Anna loves **art.** Melissa loves **music.**

Find all the art supplies.

Circle them.

Find all the musical instruments.

Draw a line under them.

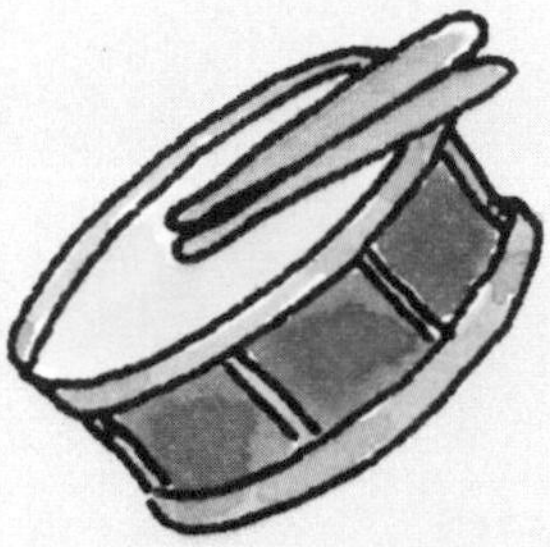

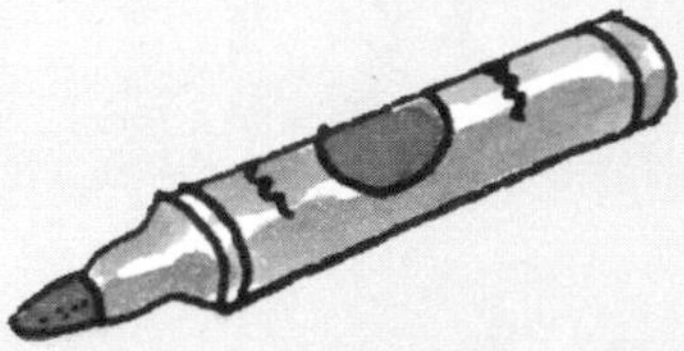

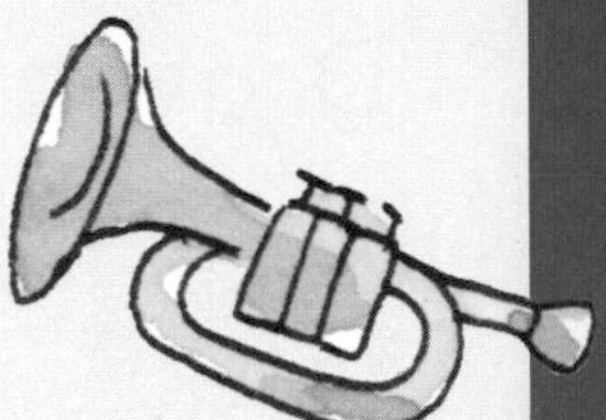

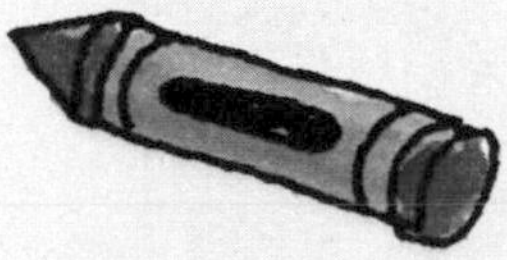

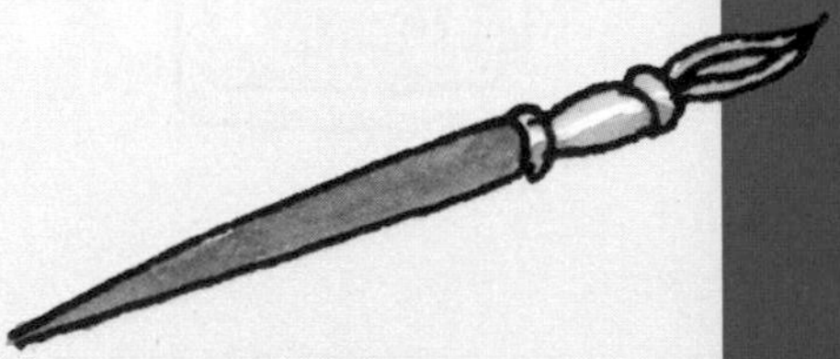

Buttons!

Buttons come in all shapes and colors.

Find the buttons that are shaped like triangles. Circle them.

Draw a line under all the blue buttons.

TIME AND MONEY

Ticktock! What time do you go to bed? How much money is in your piggy bank? Let's practice working with time and money!

PARENTS Learning can be frustrating, but you can help turn a child's struggle into a positive experience. If your learner says "I can't do this," have them add the word *yet*. Saying "I can't do this yet" sets a goal and helps them be persistent.

PLACE A STICKER HERE

For additional resources, visit www.BrainQuest.com/kindergarten

The Clock!

A **clock** has 12 numbers.

Each number stands for one **hour.**

A clock has a **big hand.**
It points to the **minutes.**

A clock has a **little hand.**
It points to the **hour.**

Color the **big hand blue.**

Color the **little hand green.**

Color each number on the clock **brown.**

Ticktock!

3:00

The **little hand** is pointing to the 3.

The **big hand** is pointing to the 12.

That means it's 3:00.

Trace the time on each clock.

1:00

2:00

3:00

4:00

5:00

6:00

7:00

8:00

9:00

10:00

11:00

12:00

The Hours!

Help the baker read the clocks.

Circle the correct time for each clock.

Watch It!

Look at the watches.

What time is it on each watch?

Draw a line to the correct time.

3:00 | 8:00 | 1:00 | 10:00

Clocks!

Some clocks show the time like this:

Other clocks show the time like this:

Draw a line to match the clocks that show the same time.

Time to Play!

These friends have soccer practice at different times.

Write the time you see on each clock.

Set the Clocks!

Read the time.

Draw the **little hand** on each clock to show the time.

12:00

3:00

1:00

11:00

4:00

8:00

6:00

5:00

10:00

9:00

7:00

2:00

Pennies!

This is a **penny**: . A penny is **money.**

A penny is worth **1 cent.**

You write 1 cent like this: **1¢.**

Help the piggy count his pennies.

Write the number of cents on each line.

____ ¢

____ ¢

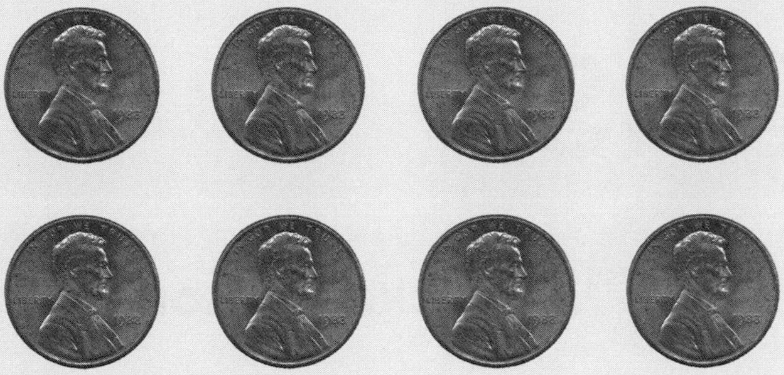

¢

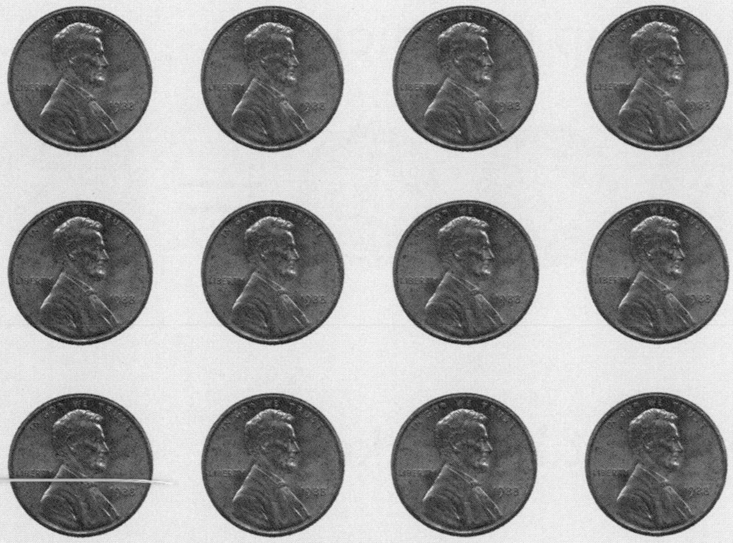

¢

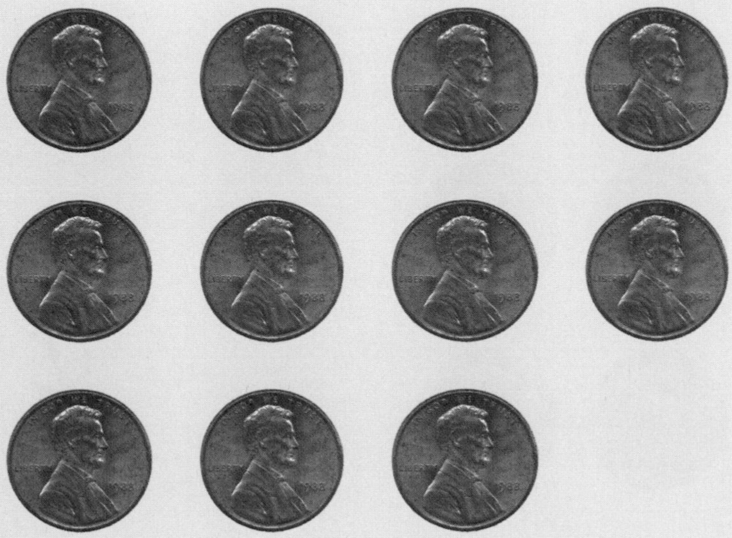

¢

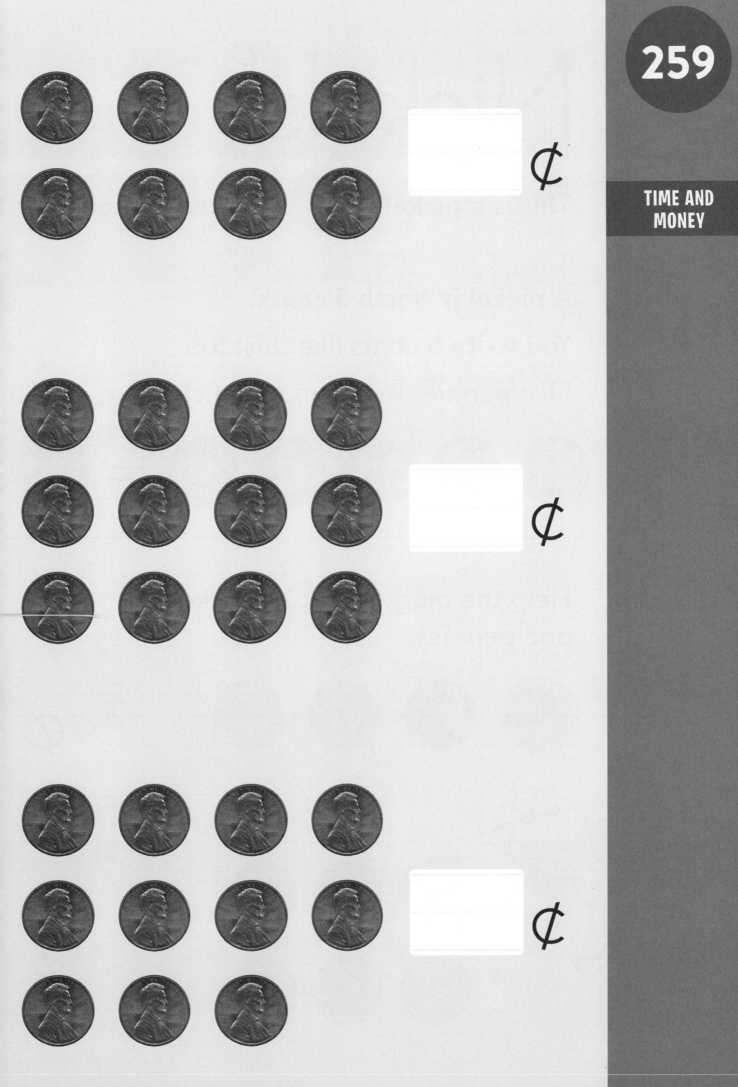

Nickels!

This is a **nickel:** . A nickel is **money.**

A nickel is worth **5 cents.**

You write 5 cents like this: **5¢.**

Five pennies make up one nickel.

Help the piggy count his nickels and pennies.

¢

¢

Dime Time!

This is a **dime:** . A dime is **money.**

A dime is worth **10 cents**, or **10¢**.

Ten pennies make up one dime.

Two nickels make up one dime.

There is one nickel. How many more pennies do you need to make a dime?

Match It!

How much money do you see?

Draw a line to match the coins to the numbers.

6¢

11¢

5¢

10¢

1¢

Lemonade!

These students sold lemonade to raise money for their school.

Circle the friend in each group who earned more money.

Save and Give!

These three sisters have been saving money.

They will donate the money to an animal shelter.

Circle the sister who has saved the most money.

COMMUNITY

Your community is the place where you live, play, and go to school. The people who live and work around us are part of our community, like crossing guards, mail carriers, and nurses. Can you name some helpers in your community?

PARENTS This section will help your child build understanding of places, people, jobs, and responsibilities in our communities. Name people and places in your community as you pass the grocery store, a local park, or the fire department. Point out the helpers.

PLACE A STICKER HERE

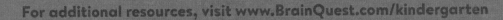

For additional resources, visit www.BrainQuest.com/kindergarten

Community

You live in a **community.**

A community is a big neighborhood.

It has lots of different places.

Look at the places in this box.

Draw a picture of a place in your community.

My Home

People live in different types of communities.

Trace the name of each community.

Some people live in:

a city.

a town.

the country.

Your Address

Your **address** tells where you live.

It tells the number of your home.

It tells the name of your street.

It tells the name of your city or town.

Write your address here.

Home Number

Street Name

Town Name

School Time

Communities have **schools.**

Schools are places to learn.

What do you like to learn in school?

Circle your favorite things.

Helpers

These are people in your community.

They have jobs that help others.

Trace the names of the people who can help you.

Who helps if you get sick?

doctor

Who helps if there is a fire?

firefighter

Who helps if you get lost?

police officer

Who helps you get mail?

mail carrier

Color their pictures.

doctor

firefighter

police officer

mail carrier

Shopping

Communities have **stores.**

Stores have things we need.

Draw a line to match each object with the correct store.

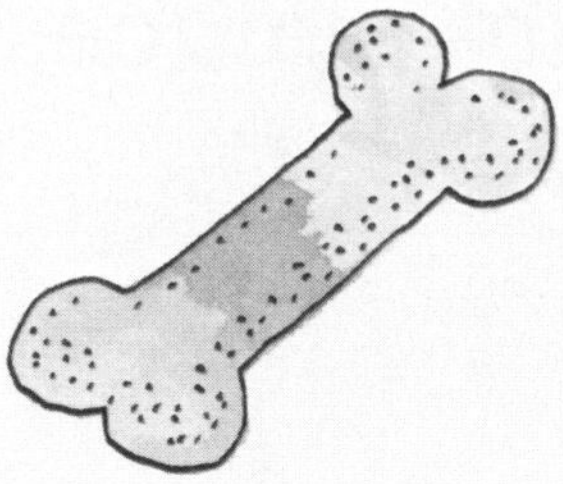

CLOTHES

TOYS

PETS

Time to Eat

Communities have places where people can buy **food.**

Circle all the places that sell food.

Clean Up!

A clean community is good for everyone.

Help clean up this community.

Draw an X through each piece of trash.

Play Time!

Communities have places to have fun.

Trace the word for each place to have fun.

Which fun places are in your community? Circle them.

park

pool

movies

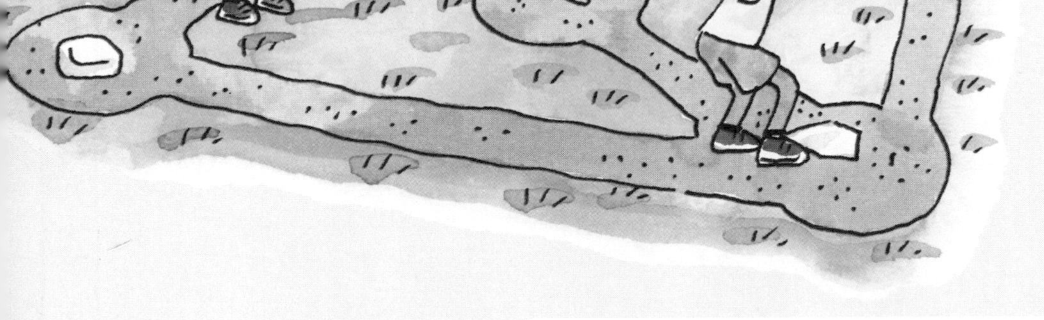

ball field

You!

Don't forget you!

What do YOU like to do in your community?

Draw a picture of yourself doing what you like to do.

SCIENCE

Plants and animals are living things—they grow and change. How have you changed since your last birthday? Are you taller? A faster runner? Let's learn more about living things in this science section.

PARENTS Our senses, the seasons, how plants grow—science for kindergartners is about being curious and building understanding of the world around them. Help your child develop curiosity and act like a scientist by encouraging them to ask questions and observe what they see at home and in your community.

For additional resources, visit www.BrainQuest.com/kindergarten

Five Senses

Your **five senses** help you learn about the world.

Draw a line from each sense word to the matching body part.

see

hear

smell

taste

touch

Which sense goes best with each picture?

Draw a line from the picture to the sense you would use.

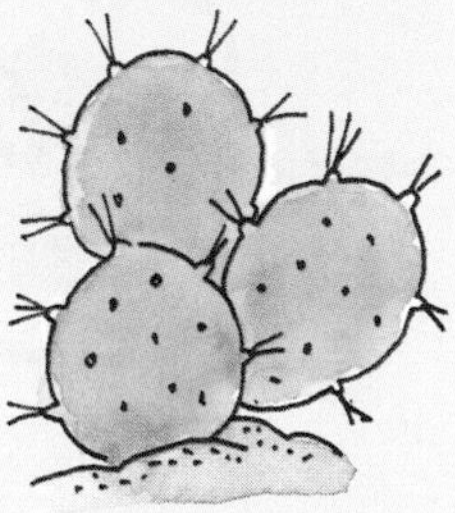
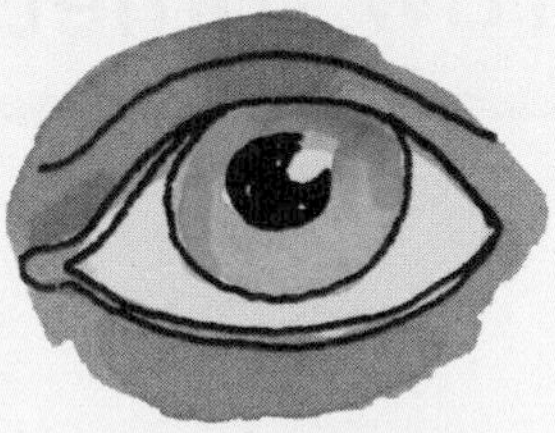

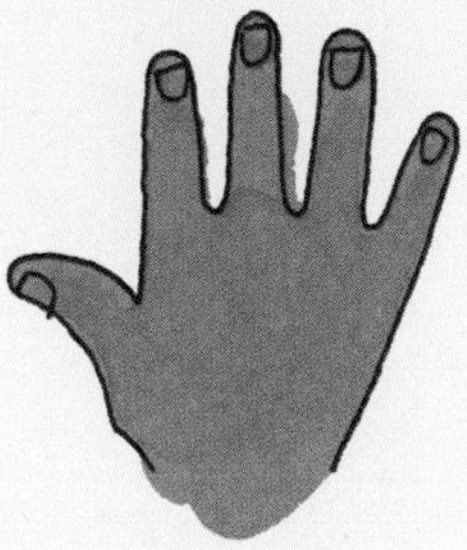

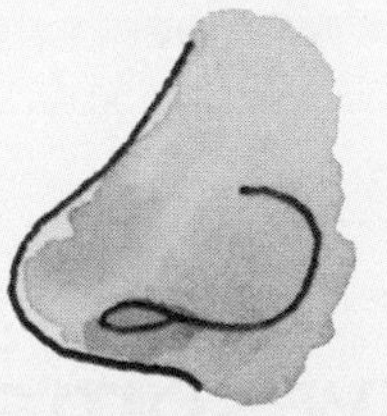

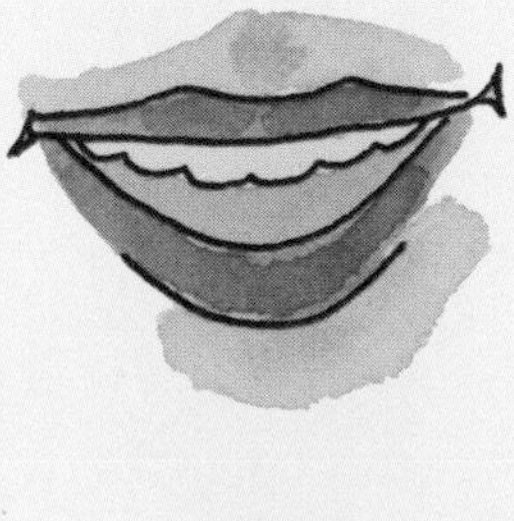

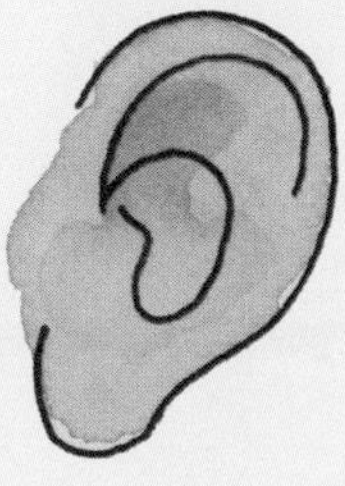

Picture It!

Use your **five senses** to draw pictures.

Draw something you **see.**

Draw something you **hear.**

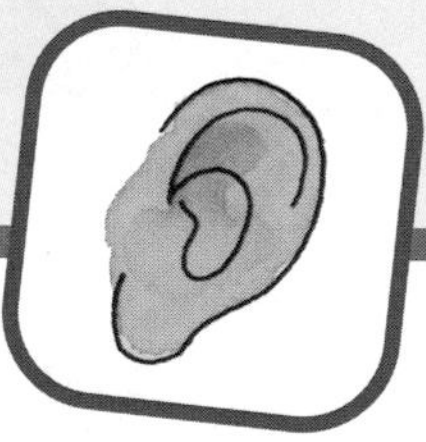

Draw something you **smell.**

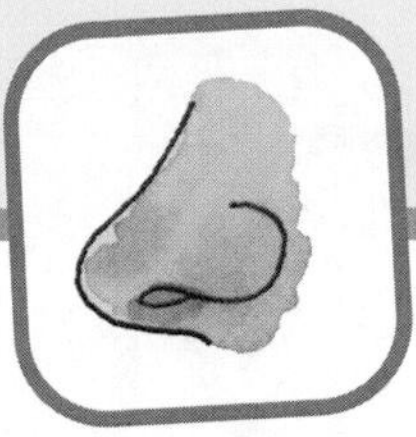

Draw something you **touch.**

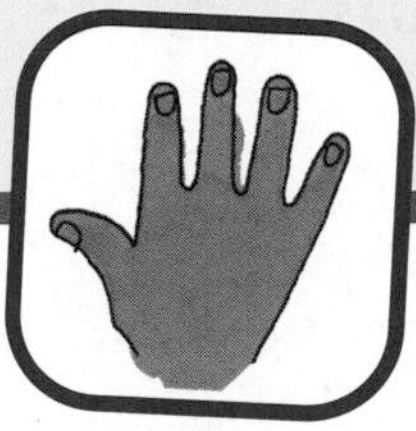

Draw something you **taste.**

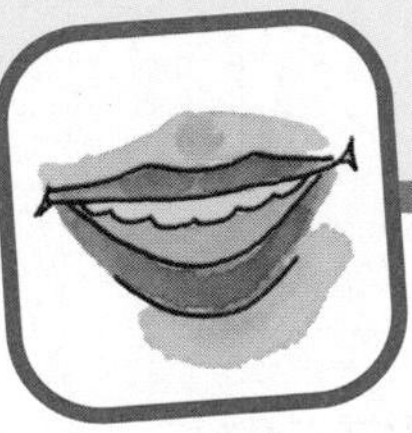

Our Earth

We live on the planet Earth.

Earth has land and water.

Color the land **green**.
Color the water **blue**.

Wear It!

Different types of **weather** need different types of clothes.

Look at each weather picture.

Circle the clothing you should wear.

Seasons

There are **four seasons.**

Look at each picture.

Draw a line to match the picture with the right season.

fall

spring

winter

summer

Weather

Read about the **weather** for each day of the week.

Draw a line to match the picture to the weather.

Monday

Today is snowy.

Tuesday

Today is rainy.

Wednesday

Today has thunderstorms.

Thursday

Today is windy.

Friday

Today is sunny.

Recycle!

People use a lot of paper.

People use a lot of bottles and cans.

We can use these things again.

We can recycle!

Draw a line from each picture to the right recycling bin.

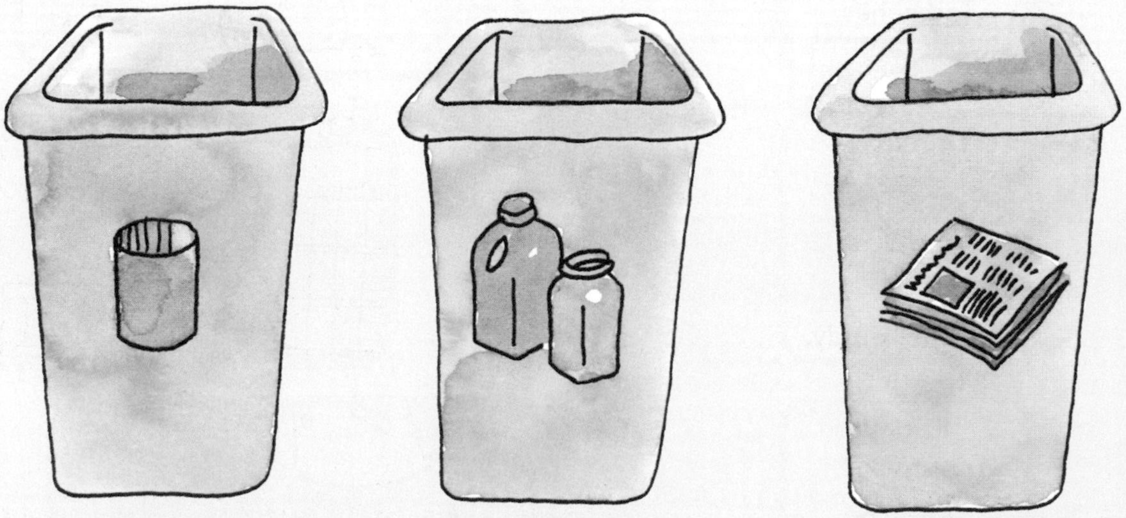

cans bottles paper

Plants

Plants are living things.

Circle the things most plants need to grow.

Growth

How do plants grow?

Number the pictures from 1 to 6 to show how a plant grows.

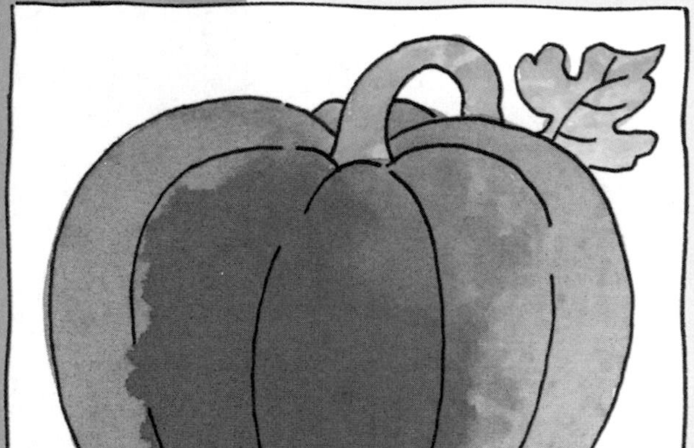

It's Living

Plants are living things. Animals are living, too. All living things need air, food, and water to live.

Look at the picture. Draw a circle around all the things that are living.

Mammals!

Mammals are animals that have fur or hair.

Look at the animals below.

Circle the mammals.

Birds and Reptiles

Birds have wings. They can fly.

Reptiles have scales. They cannot fly.

Write a B next to each bird.

Write an R next to each reptile.

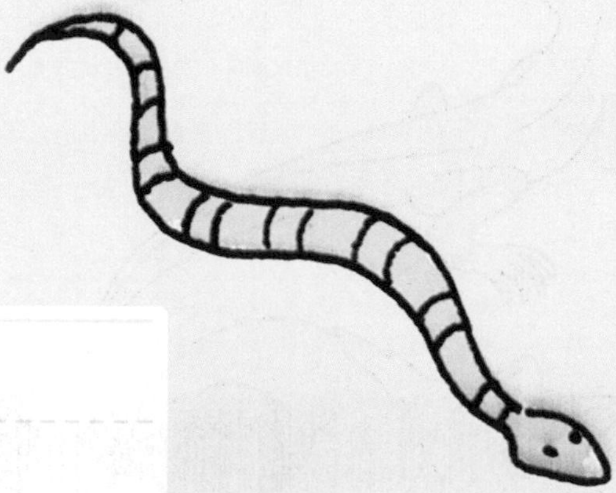

Habitats!

The place where an animal lives is called its **habitat.**

Draw a line from the animal to the matching habitat.

Oceans!

Many animals live in the ocean!

Which ocean animal is swimming here?

Connect the dots to find out.

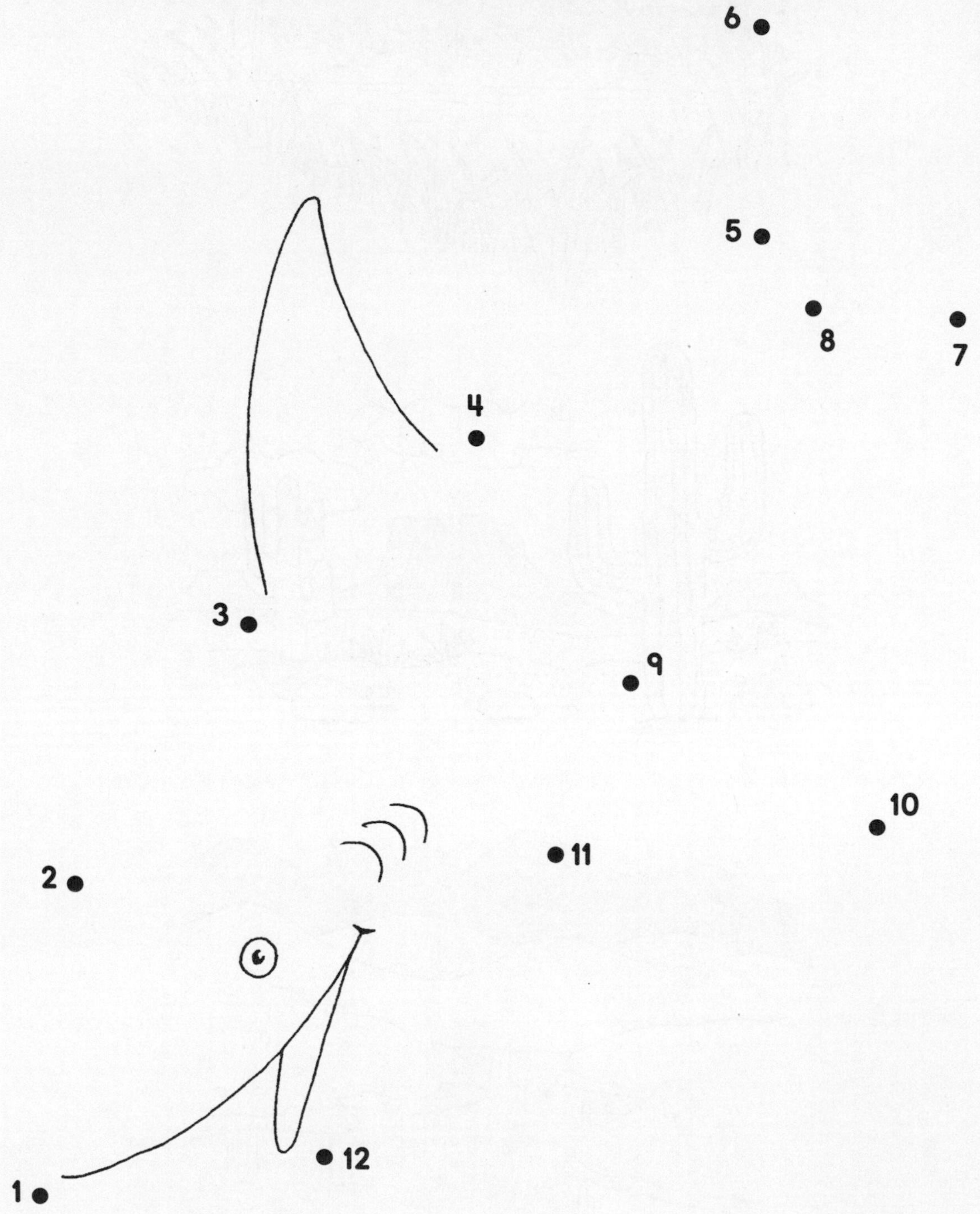

TECHNOLOGY

Technology is computers, tablets, and smartphones. It is also inventing new solutions to solve problems. Let's look at different kinds of technology and do some puzzles using skills that can help us understand how computers work.

PARENTS Help your learner connect language, math, science, and the world around them through investigations with technology. These pages include an introduction to basic computer vocabulary and puzzles that use patterns, sequence, and representation in code, laying the foundation for future learning in computer science.

PLACE A STICKER HERE

For additional resources, visit www.BrainQuest.com/kindergarten

Computer Parts

Computer hardware is any part of a computer we can see and touch. Let's find some hardware.

Circle the **screens** with a **blue** crayon.

Circle the **keyboards** with a **red** crayon.

Draw a rectangle around the **printer**.

Buttons

The buttons on a computer do different jobs. Do you know what the picture on each button means? Draw a line from the computer button to the matching action.

Faces and Shapes!

Let's play a game:

If you see a  draw a .

If you see a  draw a .

If you see a  draw a .

Now, draw the shapes to match each face.

Your Turn!

Make your own game! Draw faces first, then shapes.

TECHNOLOGY

Penguin Paths!

The penguins want to swim! Help them reach the water. Draw one arrow in each box to move the penguin one step.

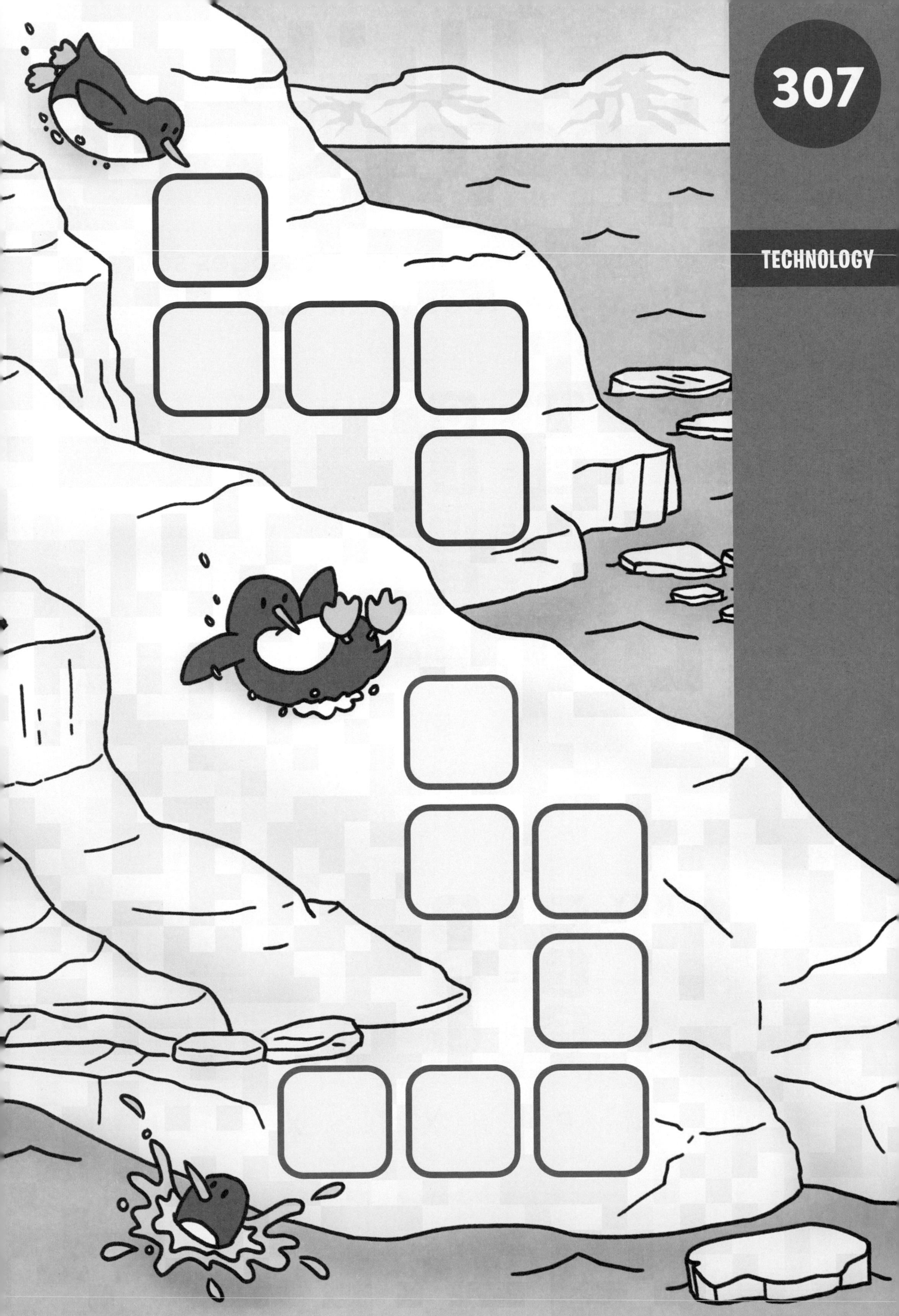

Secret Code!

What do these secret messages say?
Use the key to solve the code.

KEY

A = O
B = L
C = H
D = E

C D B B A

KEY

X = O
L = D
P = G

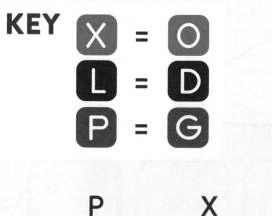

P X X L

BRAIN QUEST EXTRAS

You finished the book! Time to make a Brain Quest Mini-Deck so you can play and learn wherever you go. Write your name on your certificate and hang your progress map. Great work!
BRAIN QUEST

PARENTS Congratulations to you and your learner. In this section, you can help your child cut out a Brain Quest Mini-Deck and certificate and hang up their map. Show your child where to place the stickers and offer them praise for their achievement.

PLACE A STICKER HERE

For additional resources, visit www.BrainQuest.com/kindergarten

CONGRATULATIONS!

You've finished the Brain Quest Workbook!

All your hard work paid off! Ask a grown-up for help and cut out these SMART CARDS to make your own Brain Quest Mini-Deck.

You can play these anywhere—in the back of the car, at the park, or even at the grocery store. Remember: It's fun to be smart!

Brain Quest Mini-Deck

QUESTIONS

Find three things that are wrong with this picture.

BRAIN QUEST®

QUESTIONS

Find the circle in this picture.

How many stars do you see?

BRAIN QUEST®

QUESTIONS

Find four things that are wrong with this picture.

BRAIN QUEST®

QUESTIONS

Find four things that do not belong in the piñata.

BRAIN QUEST®

QUESTIONS

These three things are missing from the picture. Point to where they go.

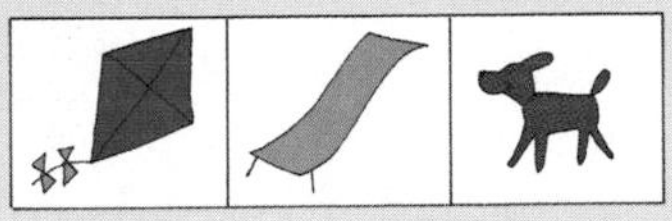

BRAIN QUEST®

QUESTIONS

Find four things that are wrong with this picture.

BRAIN QUEST®

Brain Quest Mini-Deck

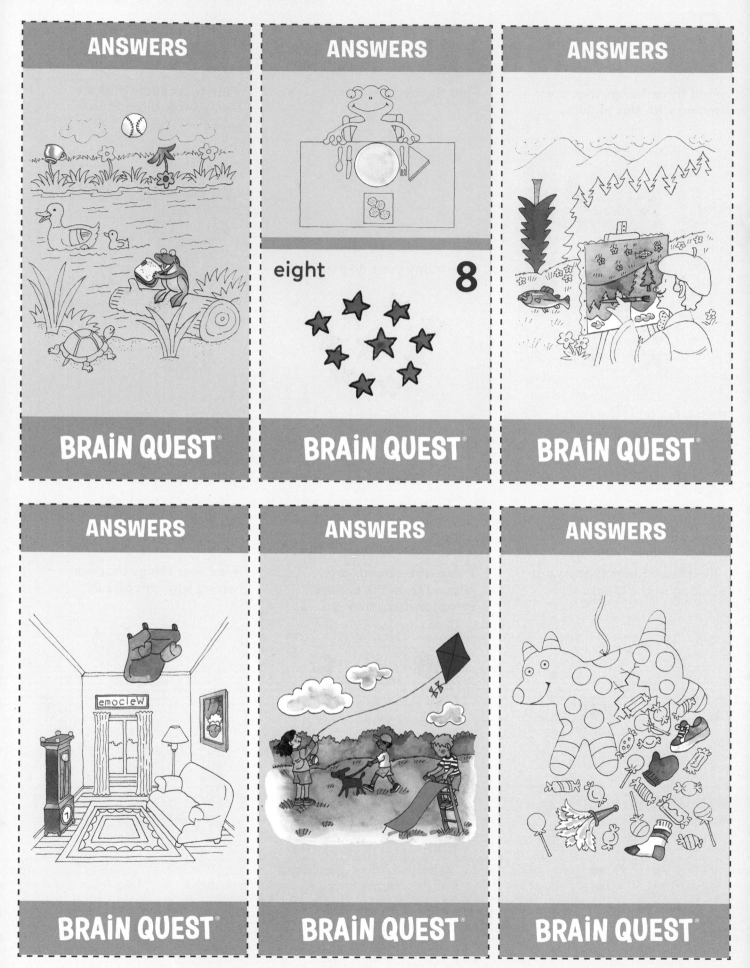

ANSWERS

BRAIN QUEST®

ANSWERS

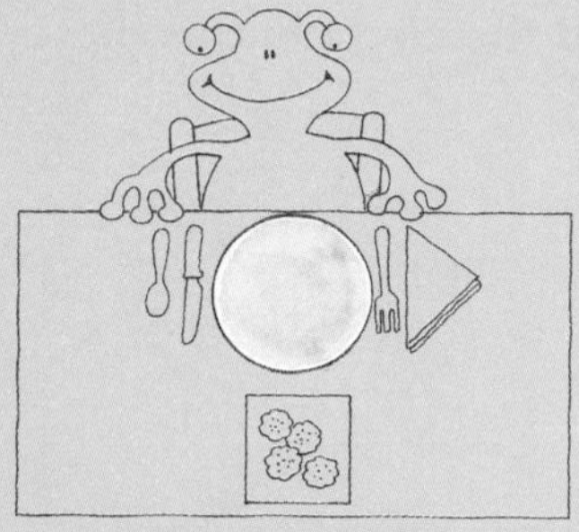

eight 8

BRAIN QUEST®

ANSWERS

BRAIN QUEST®

ANSWERS

BRAIN QUEST®

ANSWERS

BRAIN QUEST®

ANSWERS

BRAIN QUEST®

Brain Quest Mini-Deck

QUESTIONS

The cookie costs 5¢. Which coin do you need to buy it?

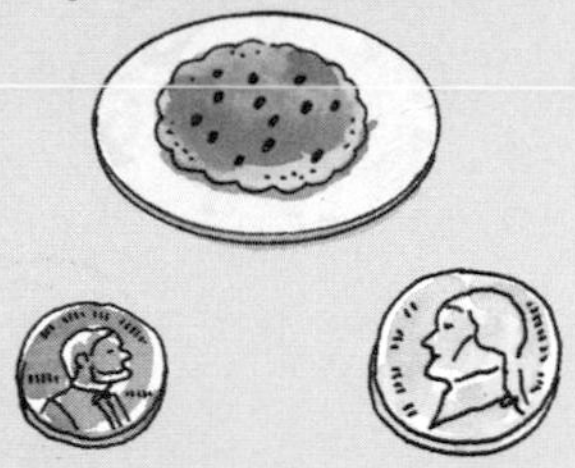

Are there more **green tops** or **yellow tops**?

BRAIN QUEST®

QUESTIONS

Look at the pattern. Which cow comes next?

Look at the pattern. Which animal comes next?

BRAIN QUEST®

QUESTIONS

Balloon, bird, kite. Which two begin with the same letter?

BRAIN QUEST®

QUESTIONS

If the squirrel eats one nut, how many nuts will be left?

BRAIN QUEST®

QUESTIONS

How many tops do you see?

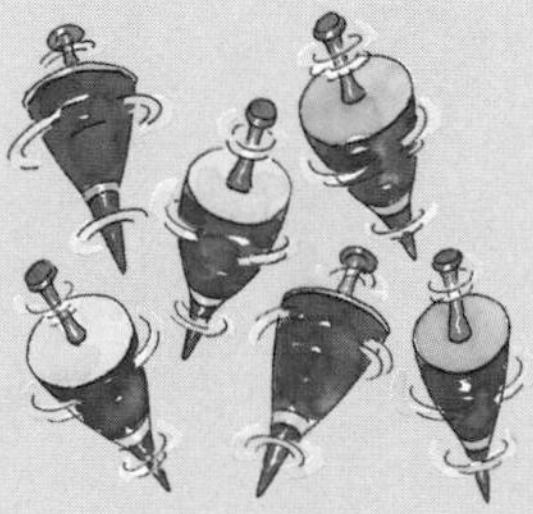

The cake costs 10¢. Which coin do you need to buy it?

BRAIN QUEST®

QUESTIONS

Slide, run, dog. Which one rhymes with **ride**?

Bird, swing, seesaw. Which one rhymes with **ring**?

BRAIN QUEST®

Brain Quest Mini-Deck

ANSWERS

b̲alloon

b̲ird

Bb

BRAIN QUEST®

ANSWERS

BRAIN QUEST®

ANSWERS

the nickel

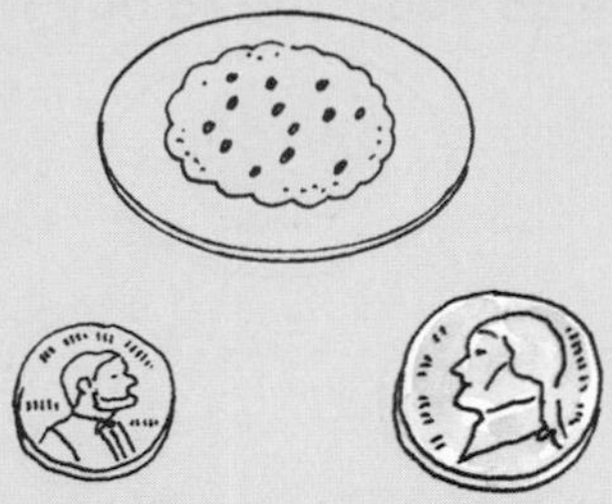

green

BRAIN QUEST®

ANSWERS

slide

swing

BRAIN QUEST®

ANSWERS

six

6

the dime

BRAIN QUEST®

ANSWERS

five

5

BRAIN QUEST®

Brain Quest Mini-Deck

QUESTIONS

Are there more **pancakes** or **muffins**?

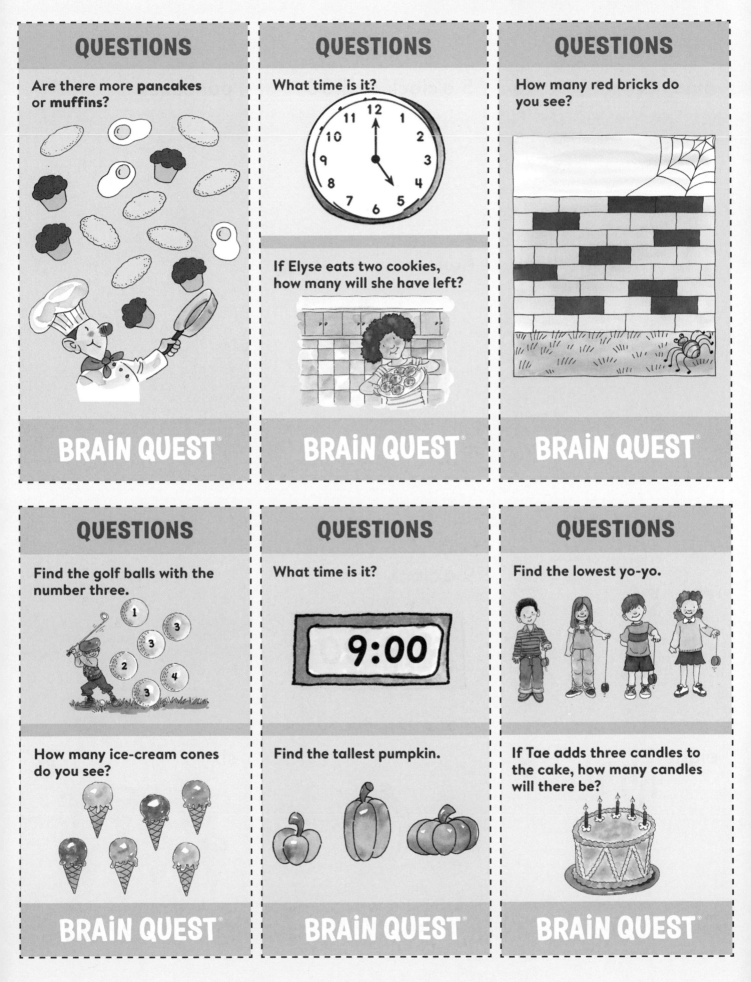

BRAIN QUEST®

QUESTIONS

What time is it?

If Elyse eats two cookies, how many will she have left?

BRAIN QUEST®

QUESTIONS

How many red bricks do you see?

BRAIN QUEST®

QUESTIONS

Find the golf balls with the number three.

How many ice-cream cones do you see?

BRAIN QUEST®

QUESTIONS

What time is it?

Find the tallest pumpkin.

BRAIN QUEST®

QUESTIONS

Find the lowest yo-yo.

If Tae adds three candles to the cake, how many candles will there be?

BRAIN QUEST®

Brain Quest Mini-Deck

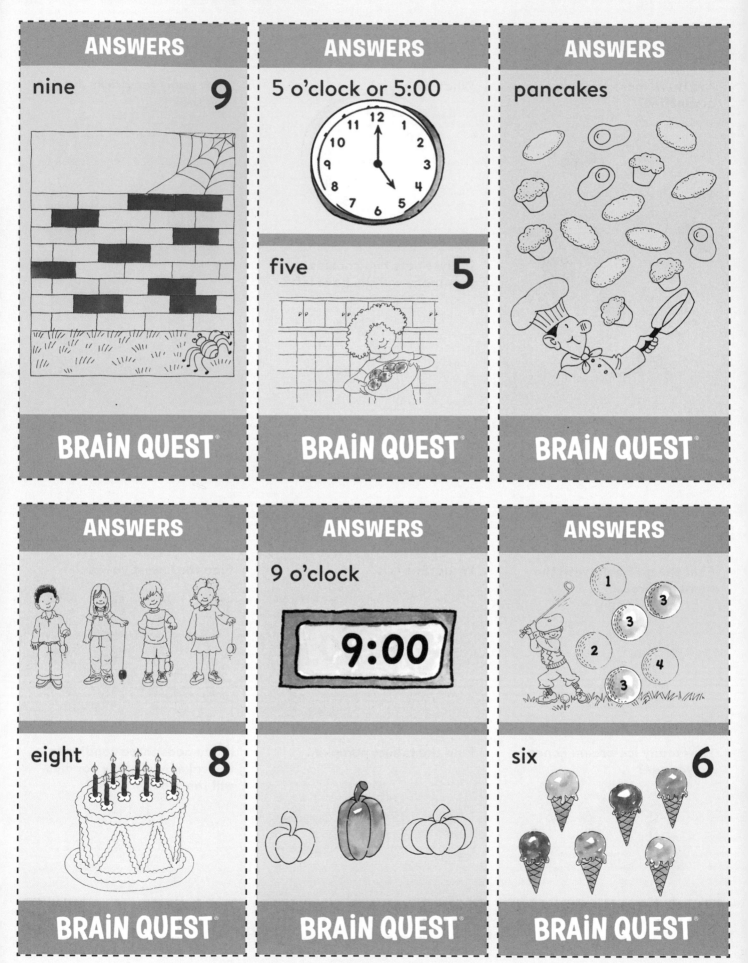

ANSWERS

nine **9**

BRAIN QUEST®

ANSWERS

5 o'clock or 5:00

five **5**

BRAIN QUEST®

ANSWERS

pancakes

BRAIN QUEST®

ANSWERS

eight **8**

BRAIN QUEST®

ANSWERS

9 o'clock

BRAIN QUEST®

ANSWERS

six **6**

BRAIN QUEST®

Brain Quest Mini-Deck

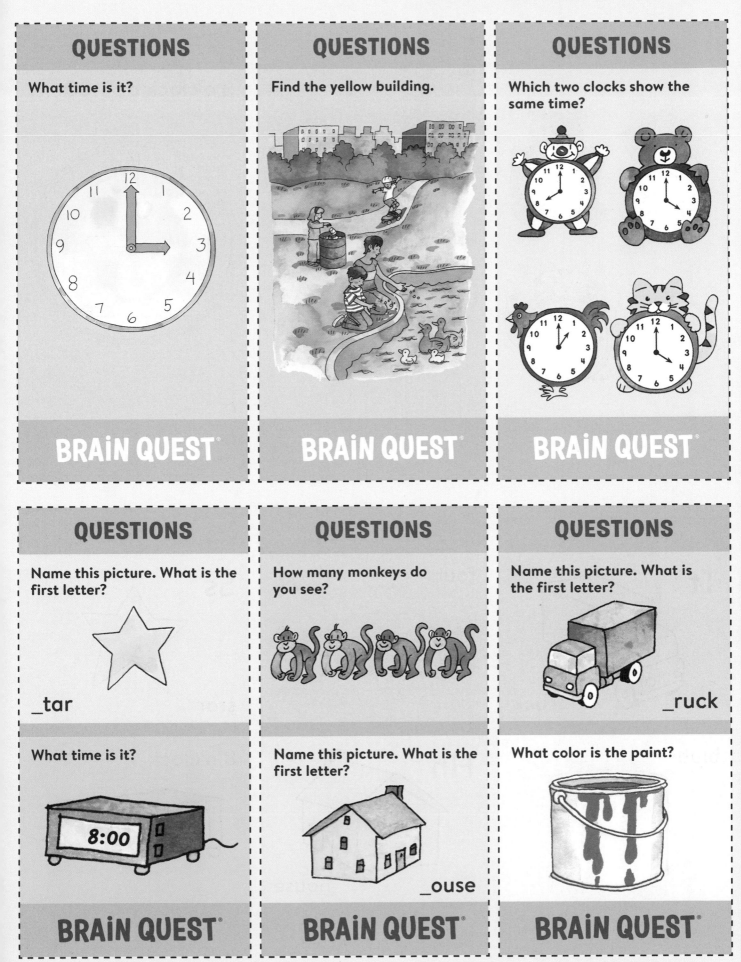

QUESTIONS

What time is it?

BRAIN QUEST®

QUESTIONS

Find the yellow building.

BRAIN QUEST®

QUESTIONS

Which two clocks show the same time?

BRAIN QUEST®

QUESTIONS

Name this picture. What is the first letter?

_tar

What time is it?

BRAIN QUEST®

QUESTIONS

How many monkeys do you see?

Name this picture. What is the first letter?

_ouse

BRAIN QUEST®

QUESTIONS

Name this picture. What is the first letter?

_ruck

What color is the paint?

BRAIN QUEST®

Brain Quest Mini-Deck

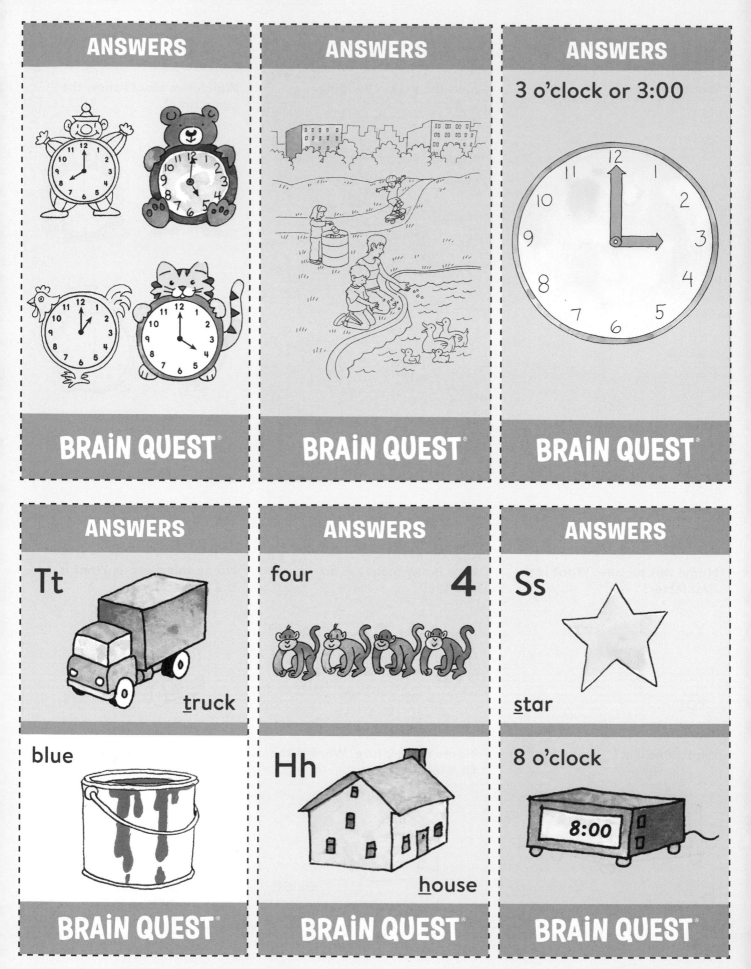

ANSWERS

BRAIN QUEST®

ANSWERS

BRAIN QUEST®

ANSWERS

3 o'clock or 3:00

BRAIN QUEST®

ANSWERS

Tt

truck

blue

BRAIN QUEST®

ANSWERS

four 4

Hh

house

BRAIN QUEST®

ANSWERS

Ss

star

8 o'clock

BRAIN QUEST®

YOU DID IT!

CONGRATULATIONS!

You completed every activity in the Brain Quest Kindergarten Workbook. Cut out the certificate (ask an adult for help!) and write your name on it. Show your friends! Hang it on your wall! You should feel proud of your hard work.

CERTIFICATE OF ACHIEVEMENT

Earned by

____

for completing all sections in the

BRAIN QUEST®

KINDERGARTEN WORKBOOK

I DID IT!
YAY!
Awesome!
WAY TO GO!
I am proud of me!
HARD WORK AHEAD
I CAN DO IT!
Brainiac!
IT'S FUN TO BE SMART!®
I DID IT!
YAY!
Awesome!
WAY TO GO!
I am proud of me!
HARD WORK AHEAD
I CAN DO IT!
Brainiac!
IT'S FUN TO BE SMART!®
I DID IT!
YAY!
Awesome!
WAY TO GO!
I am proud of me!
HARD WORK AHEAD
I CAN DO IT!
Brainiac!
IT'S FUN TO BE SMART!®

I DID IT!
YAY!
Awesome!
WAY TO GO!
I am proud of me!
HARD WORK AHEAD
I CAN DO IT!
Brainiac!
IT'S FUN TO BE SMART!®
I DID IT!
YAY!
Awesome!
WAY TO GO!
I am proud of me!
HARD WORK AHEAD
I CAN DO IT!
Brainiac!
IT'S FUN TO BE SMART!®
I DID IT!
YAY!
Awesome!
WAY TO GO!
I am proud of me!
HARD WORK AHEAD
I CAN DO IT!
Brainiac!
IT'S FUN TO BE SMART!®